Lab Manual for

Security+ Guide to Network Security Fundamentals

Paul Cretaro

THOMSON

COURSE TECHNOLOGY

Australia • Canada • Mexico • Singapore • Spain • United Kingdom • United States

THOMSON

COURSE TECHNOLOGY

Lab Manual for Security+ Guide to Network Security Fundamentals
by Paul Cretaro

Senior Editor:
William Pitkin III

Product Manager:
Laura Hildebrand

Developmental Editor:
Dave George

Production Editor:
Brooke Booth

Technical Editor:
Rob Andrews

Senior Manufacturing Coordinator:
Laura Burns

Quality Assurance Technical Lead:
Nicole Ashton

Marketing Manager:
Jason Sakos

Associate Product Manager:
Tim Gleeson

Editorial Assistant:
Nick Lombardi

Text Designer:
GEX Publishing Services

Compositor:
GEX Publishing Services

Cover Design:
Julie Malone

TABLE OF CONTENTS

INTRODUCTION

Hands-on learning is the best way to master security skills necessary for both CompTIA's Security+ Exam and for a network security career. This book contains hands-on exercises that apply fundamental networking concepts as they would be applied in the real world. In addition, each chapter offers review questions to reinforce your mastery of network security topics. The organization of this book follows the same organization as Course Technology's *Security+ Guide to Network Security Fundamentals*, and using the two together will provide a substantial, effective learning experience. This book is suitable for use in a beginning or intermediate networking course. As a prerequisite, students should have a fundamental understanding of general networking concepts, and at least one course in network operating systems. This book is best used when accompanied by the Course Technology textbook *Security+ Guide to Network Security Fundamentals*, or another Security+ textbook.

FEATURES

In order to ensure a successful experience for instructors and students alike, this book includes the following features:

- **Security+ Certification Objectives:** Each chapter lists the relevant objectives from the CompTIA Security+ Exam.
- **Lab Objectives:** Every lab has a brief description and list of learning objectives.
- **Materials Required:** Every lab includes information on network access privileges, hardware, software, and other materials you will need to complete the lab.
- **Completion Times:** Every lab has an estimated completion time, so that you can plan your activities more accurately.
- **Activity Sections:** Labs are presented in manageable sections. Where appropriate, additional activity background information is provided to illustrate the importance of a particular project.
- **Step-by-Step Instructions:** Logical and precise step-by-step instructions guide you through the hands-on activities in each lab.
- **Review Questions:** Questions help reinforce concepts presented in the lab.

Note for instructors: Answers to review questions are available on the Course Technology Web site at www.course.com. Search on this book's ISBN, which is found on the back cover.

HARDWARE REQUIREMENTS

The following list gives the hardware required to complete all of the labs in the book. Many of the individual labs require less hardware than listed below.

- Three computers with Pentium 166 MHz CPU or higher processors (400 MHz recommended) with the following features:
  - 128 MB of RAM minimum (256 MB recommended) in each computer
  - A 4 GB hard disk with at least 1 GB of available storage space (10 GB hard disk or larger with at least 7 GB available storage space recommended) in each computer
  - A CD-ROM drive
- Internet access
- Two PCI Ethernet network interface cards for each PC
- A hub or switch
- At least 4 Category 5 UTP straight-through patch cables
- At least 2 Category 5 UTP crossover patch cables
- A Cisco 1900 switch
- A proprietary Cisco console port cable
- An RJ-45-to-DB-9 or DB-25 adapter
- A Cisco Aironet 340

SOFTWARE/SETUP REQUIREMENTS

- At least two copies of Windows 2000 Server with Windows 2000 Service Pack 3
- Microsoft IIS Version 5 installed on Windows 2000 Server
- Internet Explorer 6 Web browser
- PGP
- Outlook Express
- An anonymous e-mailer*
- Bastion.inf security configuration file*
- ZDelete Auto Cleaner*
- Restorer2000*
- Snort 1.8.x*
- WinPcap*

- IDSCenter*
- BackOfficer*
- IISLockdown Tool
- Microsoft Baseline Security Analyzer

These programs may be downloaded from the vendor Web site.

CLASSROOM SETUP GUIDELINES

Instructor PC

1. Partitions
   a. C:\ 3GB NTFS
   b. D:\ 4GB FAT32
2. Windows 2000 Server Installation
   a. Boot to the Windows 2000 Server CD
   b. Press F8 to Accept the license agreement
   c. Create a 3GB partition
   d. Format the partition using NTFS
   e. Set Regional settings if necessary
   f. Enter your name and company
   g. Enter the Product key
   h. Select Per Seat licensing
   i. Computer Name: Instructor
   j. Administrator Password: password
   k. Adjust the time zone if necessary
   l. Custom Network Settings:
       Configure TCP/IP settings with:

       i. IP address: 192.168.x.100 – Note: replace x with the classroom number

       ii. Subnet Mask: 255.255.255.0

       iii. DNS Server 192.168.x.100

       iv. Accept WORKGROUP as the Workgroup

3. Active Directory setup:
   a. Run dcpromo
   b. Create a new domain, tree, forest
   c. Let the Active Directory installation install DNS
   d. DNS name: Class.dom
   e. Accept default settings
4. DNS Setup:
   a. Enable dynamic updates on the Class.dom Zone
   b. Create a standard primary Reverse lookup zone for 192.168.x
   c. Enable Dynamic updates
   d. DHCP setup
   e. Scope name: Class
   f. IP range: 192.168.x.1–254
   g. Subnet Mask: 255.255.255.0
   h. Exclusions: 192.168.x.1–20, 192.168.x.100–254
   i. Configure Options:
      i. Router: 192.168.x.100
      ii. Domain Name: Class.dom
      iii. DNS server: 192.168.x.100

STUDENT PC

1. Partitions
   a. C:\ 3GB NTFS
   b. D:\ 4GB FAT32
2. Windows 2000 Server Installation
   a. Boot to the Windows 2000 Server CD
   b. Press F8 to Accept the license agreement
   c. Create a 3GB partition
   d. Format the partition using NTFS
   e. Set Regional settings if necessary
   f. Enter your name and company
   g. Enter the Product key

h. Select Per Seat licensing

i. Computer Name: Server-x Note: replace x with a number assigned by your instructor.

j. Administrator Password: password

k. Adjust the time zone if necessary

l. Accept the typical Network Settings

ACKNOWLEDGMENTS

I would like to thank Course Technology for giving me the opportunity to write this lab manual. I would also like to thank Dave George and Laura Hildebrand for being indispensable resources. Thanks also to all the peer reviewers who worked under very tight deadlines and gave great feedback: Mike Parsons, Mike Casper, Mike Daveler, Amelia Phillips, and Rob Andrews. Finally, I'd like to thank my wonderful wife Sherrie and my three boys, Mark, Michael, and Adam, for their support and patience. Finally, thanks to Buddie, my dog, for keeping me company when everyone else was asleep.

SECURITY OVERVIEW

Labs included in this chapter:

➤ Lab 1.1 Using NTFS to Secure Local Resources

➤ Lab 1.2 Data Confidentiality

➤ Lab 1.3 Data Availability

➤ Lab 1.4 Data Integrity

➤ Lab 1.5 Data Encryption

CompTIA Security+ Exam Objectives	
Objective	**Lab**
General Security Concepts: Access Control	1.1, 1.2, 1.3, 1.4, 1.5

LAB 1.1 USING NTFS TO SECURE LOCAL RESOURCES

Objectives

Local computer security, especially at the file level, is often ignored. Most people are familiar with the Windows 9x version of Microsoft Windows, which uses FAT and does not offer local file security. NTFS, the file system for Windows NT/2000, is designed with local file security in mind. To take advantage of these capabilities, you must have Windows NT, 2000, or XP with the NTFS file system installed. It is important to note that although all of these operating systems are compatible with FAT, local file security will be enabled only if you have NTFS installed.

After completing this lab, you will be able to:

➤ Determine if a partition is FAT or NTFS

➤ Convert a FAT partition to NTFS

Materials Required

This lab will require the following:

➤ A computer running Windows 2000 Server as a standalone or member server

➤ Administrative access to the server

➤ At least one partition formatted with FAT or FAT32

Estimated completion time: **10 minutes**

ACTIVITY

1. Log on to the Windows 2000 server as Administrator.
2. Click **Start**.
3. Click **Run**.
4. Type **cmd** to invoke the command line.

The FAT partition in this lab will be designated as drive letter E.

5. At the command line type **chkntfs e:** to verify that the drive is not using NTFS. You will see the message, "E: is not dirty". This means that there is no corruption on the drive.
6. At the command line type **convert e: /fs:ntfs** to convert the FAT partition to NTFS.

7. If the drive has a volume label, enter it when prompted. Windows will then convert the drive to NTFS. Note: If you convert the system partition you will have to reboot for the conversion to take place.

8. At the command line type **chkntfs e:** to verify that the drive is now NTFS.

9. An example of the steps is shown in Figure 1-1.

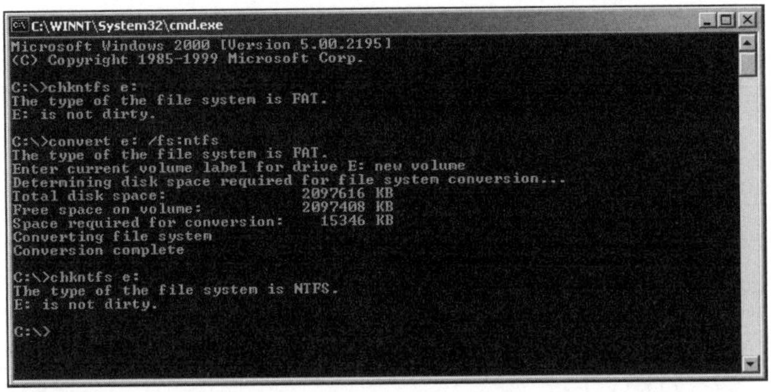

Figure 1-1   Using the CHKNTFS and CONVERT commands

10. Close all Windows and log off.

Certification Objectives

Objectives for CompTIA Security + Exam:

➤ General Security Concepts: Access Control

Review Questions

1. What file systems are compatible with Windows NT 4.0?

   a. FAT

   b. FAT32

   c. OSPF

   d. NTFS

2. Which of the following are features of NTFS version 5 that are not available with FAT partitions?

   a. Share Level Security

   b. File Level Security

   c. Compression

   d. Encryption

3. Which of the following commands will convert a FAT partition to NTFS?

    a. update C: /FS:NTFS

    b. upgrade C: /FS:NTFS

    c. convert C: /FS:NTFS

    d. convert C: /NTFS

4. What are the permissions available for Windows folder shares?

    a. Read

    b. Modify

    c. Change

    d. Full Control

5. Once a FAT partition has been converted to NTFS, the only way to change it back to FAT is to rebuild the drive and restore from a backup. True or False?

LAB 1.2 DATA CONFIDENTIALITY

Objectives

Once a secure file system is installed, you can begin to think about data confidentiality. Data confidentiality refers to making sure that only those intended to have access to certain data actually have that access. With the FAT file system, this is not possible at the local level, but with NTFS you can lock down both folders and files locally. NTFS can be used to protect data from intruders who may have physical access to the computer containing the data. In this lab, you will create a folder and files, assign NTFS permissions, then verify whether or not the data is confidential.

After completing this lab, you will be able to:

➤ Assign NTFS Permissions to the folder and files to secure local resources

➤ Verify that the data is confidential

Materials Required

This lab will require the following:

➤ A computer running Windows 2000 Server as a standalone or member server

➤ Administrative access to the server

➤ An NTFS partition

➤ Two user-level accounts: User1 and User2

Estimated completion time: **15 minutes**

ACTIVITY

1. Log on to the Windows 2000 server as Administrator.

2. Open My Computer, and then double-click on the E: drive. This should be the drive that was converted from FAT to NTFS in Lab 1.1.

3. Create a new folder called **Confidentiality**.

4. Double-click the Confidentiality folder and create a new folder called **User1Folder**.

5. To secure this folder from other users, right-click **User1Folder**.

6. Click **Properties** to open the User1Folder Properties window.

7. Click the **Security** tab, as seen in Figure 1-2. Note: if the drive was not formatted with NTFS the Security tab will be unavailable.

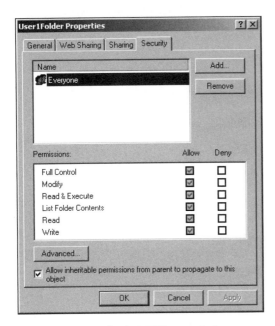

Figure 1-2   Default NTFS permissions

8. Uncheck the box "Allow inheritable permissions from parent to propagate to this object".

9. You will receive the message shown in Figure 1-3.

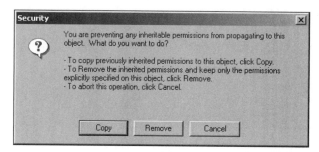

Figure 1-3   The Security warning when changing the default NTFS permissions

10. Click **Copy** to retain the permissions.

11. Click **Add** and the Select Users, Computers, or Groups window will pop up.

12. Make sure your server is selected in the **Look in** drop down box.

13. Select **User1**, then click **Add**.

14. Click **OK**.

15. With User1 still highlighted, click the **Allow Full Control** box.

16. Click the name **Everyone**, then click **Remove**. The screen will resemble the one in Figure 1-4.

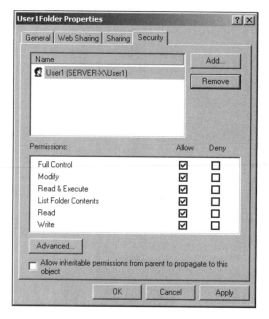

Figure 1-4   User1 permissions after the default NTFS permissions were removed

17. Click **OK**.

18. Double-click **User1Folder**. Your access should be denied because you only granted User1 access.

19. Close all windows and log off.

20. Log on as User1 and navigate to the User1Folder to verify that the user has access to the folder. You should be able to access the folder.

21. Close all windows and log off.

Certification Objectives

Objectives for CompTIA Security + Exam:

> ➤ General Security Concepts: Access Control

Review Questions

1. The best way to define data confidentiality is:

   a. data that has not been tampered with intentionally or accidentally

   b. data that has been scrambled for remote transmission

   c. data that is secured so only the intended people have access

   d. data that can be accessed when it is needed

2. When comparing the Full Control and Modify NTFS permissions, what differentiates the two?

   a. Full Control is exactly the same as Modify.

   b. Full Control allows you to change permissions and ownership.

   c. Modify only allows changes, while Full Control allows changes as well as deletions.

   d. Modify allows you to change permissions and ownership.

3. A safeguard in Windows NT/2000 allows administrators to access data even if they have been explicitly denied. How is this possible?

   a. Administrators can take ownership and change the permissions to allow access.

   b. Administrators can log on as a user with permissions and grant themselves access.

   c. Administrators cannot be denied access to data.

   d. This safeguard does not exist; Administrators can be denied access to data.

4. When NTFS permissions are combined with other NTFS permissions what are the effective permissions?

   a. most restrictive

   b. least restrictive

5. When NTFS permissions are combined with Share permissions, what are the effective permissions?

   a. most restrictive

   b. least restrictive

LAB 1.3 DATA AVAILABILITY

Objectives

Although it is important that data remains secure and confidential, it is just as important that the data is available when needed. Secured data that is inaccessible is considered downtime and detrimental to a business and its ability to serve customers. Technologies such as clustering and load balancing can help, but if NTFS permissions are assigned inappropriately, these features will not help.

After completing this lab, you will be able to:

➤ Share data so that it is available to those that require access

➤ Understand how confidentiality and availability work together

Materials required

This lab will require the following:

➤ A computer running Windows 2000 Server as a standalone or member server

➤ Administrative access to the server

➤ An NTFS partition

➤ Two user-level accounts: User1 and User2

Estimated completion time: **15 minutes**

ACTIVITY

1. Log on to the Windows 2000 server as Administrator.

2. Open **My Computer**, then double-click on the **E** drive.

3. Create a new folder called **Availability**.

4. Double-click the **Availability** folder and create the folder **User2Folder**.

5. Right-click on **User2Folder**.

6. Click **Properties** and the User2Folder Properties window will open.

7. Click the **Security** tab.

8. Uncheck the box "Allow inheritable permissions from parent to propagate to this object".

9. You will be prompted to Copy, Remove, or Cancel.

10. Click **Remove** to clear the permissions.

11. Click **Add** and the Select Users, Computers, or Groups window will open.

12. Make sure your server is selected in the **Look in** drop down box.

13. Select **User2**, then click **Add**.

14. Click **OK**.

15. With User2 still highlighted, click the **Allow Full Control** box.

16. Click **OK**.

17. Close all windows and log off.

18. Log on as User2 and verify that you have access to **e:\Availability\User2Folder**.

19. Close all windows and log off.

20. Log on as Administrator and delete the **User2** account from the local security database.

21. Create a new user, also named **User2**, then log off.

22. Logon as User2 and try to access the **e:\Availability\User2Folder**. Access should be denied.

23. Log off User2.

24. Log on as Administrator.

25. Check the **Security properties** of the **e:\Availability\User2Folder**. Notice the account is no longer listed, but the old SID is. Your properties should look like those in Figure 1-5.

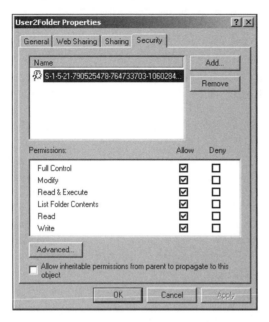

Figure 1-5   An example of permissions assigned to an account that has been deleted

26. You should be denied access. The data is no longer available to User2.

27. To verify this, log on as User2 and try to open the User2Folder. You will be denied access.

28. Close all windows and log off.

Certification Objectives

Objectives for CompTIA Security + Exam:

➤ General Security Concepts: Access Control

Review Questions

1. The best way to define data availability is:

   a. data that has not been tampered with intentionally or accidentally

   b. data that has been scrambled for remote transmission

   c. data that is secured so only the intended people have access

   d. data that can be accessed when it is needed

2. What technologies can be used to help reduce downtime and increase the time data is readily available? (Choose all that apply.)

   a. backups

   b. clustering

   c. load balancing

   d. RAID

3. A user took a leave of absence from your company for personal reasons. A junior administrator deleted the user's account from Active Directory. To fix the problem, the junior administrator re-created the account. When the user returned to work, he could not access any of his files. What is the cause?

   a. Accounts with the same name should work; that is not the cause of the problem.

   b. The user's account had expired.

   c. The user's password did not comply with the Domain Security Policy.

   d. Even though the two accounts have the same name, the SIDs are different.

4. How can data confidentiality affect data availability?

   a. They are two independent areas and do not affect each other.

   b. For data to be available, it cannot be confidential.

   c. Data that is secured too strongly may conflict with the availability.

   d. Data that is secured too weakly may conflict with the availability.

5. What percentage of downtime would be acceptable for an e-commerce business?

   a. 95%

   b. 100%

   c. 0%

   d. 50%

LAB 1.4 DATA INTEGRITY

Objectives

Once data is secured properly and available to the appropriate people, it is important to make sure that the contents of the data have not been altered accidentally or intentionally. Malicious corruption is a problem, and can be done by a virus, worm, or hacker. Accidental changes, however, can also damage data integrity. For example, Windows 2000 file synchronization capabilities could easily lead to accidental corruption. Changes made to data that conflict with other changes to the same data can damage data integrity just as much as a hacker can.

After completing this lab, you will be able to:

➤ Understand the importance of data integrity

➤ Identify potential threats to data integrity

Materials required

This lab will require the following:

➤ A computer running Windows 2000 Server as a standalone or member server

➤ An NTFS partition

➤ Two user-level accounts: User1 and User2

Estimated completion time: **10 minutes**

ACTIVITY

1. Log on to the Windows 2000 server as User1.

2. Open **My Computer**, then double-click the **E** drive.

3. Create a new folder called **Integrity**.

4. Double-click the **Integrity** folder and create a new folder called **User1Folder**.

5. Double-click the **User1Folder** folder.

6. Create a new Text document and edit the contents to say: **This document has not been modified accidentally or intentionally.**

7. Save the file as **New Text Document** and close the document.

8. Log off User1.

9. Log on as User2.

10. Navigate to the **e:\integrity\User1Folder** and remove the word "not" from the New Text Document. Because you did not assign permissions to e:\integrity\User1Folder, you can modify the contents of the file.

11. Close the file and save the changes.

The New Text Document still exists but has been modified intentionally to damage the integrity.

12. Log off User2.

Certification Objectives

Objectives for CompTIA Security + Exam:

➤ General Security Concepts: Access Control

Review Questions

1. The best way to define data integrity is:

   a. data that has not been tampered with intentionally or accidentally

   b. data that has been scrambled for remote transmission

   c. data that is secured so only the intended people have access

   d. data that can be accessed when it is needed

2. Data integrity can be damaged by which of the following? (Choose all that apply.)

   a. viruses

   b. worms

   c. hackers

   d. trojan horses

3. An Administrator restores a folder of files at the request of the owner of the folder. Two days later the user calls the Help Desk to complain that some data is missing from files that were updated two weeks ago. What could have happened?

   a. The restore failed and corrupted the data.

   b. The restore was successful but restored some files that should not have been restored.

   c. The original backup was corrupt.

   d. The user was infected with a virus.

4. Data Integrity can also be threatened by environmental hazards such as dust, surges, and excessive heat. True or False?

5. Which of the following will help maintain data integrity?

   a. disaster recovery plans

   b. an equipment standards policy

   c. system documentation

   d. preventive maintenance

LAB 1.5 DATA ENCRYPTION

Objectives

With NTFS you are not limited to folder- and file-level security. Another function of NTFS is the ability to encrypt data. Encryption is the process of taking readable data and making it unreadable. Encryption is commonly used for remote data transfer, but it can also be used for local security. Laptop users may want to use NTFS to secure and encrypt their data in the event that the laptop is stolen. While this solution is not 100% effective, it does make it more difficult to hack into your system. Windows 2000 offers a very easy way to encrypt files on an NTFS partition.

After completing this lab, you will be able to:

➤ Encrypt files on NTFS partitions

➤ Understand who has access to encrypted data

Materials Required

This lab will require the following:

➤ A computer running Windows 2000 Server as a standalone or member server

➤ Administrative access to the server

➤ An NTFS partition

➤ Two user-level accounts: User1 and User2

Estimated completion time: **15 minutes**

ACTIVITY

1. Log on to the Windows 2000 server as Administrator.

2. Open **My Computer**, then double-click the **E** drive.

3. Create a new folder called **Encryption**.

4. Double-click the **Encryption** folder and create a new folder called **User2Folder**.

5. Double-click the **User2Folder** folder.

6. Create a new text document and edit the contents to say: **This document is for my eyes only.**

7. Save the document as **Private Document.txt** and close the document.

8. Right-click on the document.

9. Select **Properties**.

10. Click the **Advanced** button.

11. Check the **Encrypt contents to secure data** box, as shown in Figure 1-6.

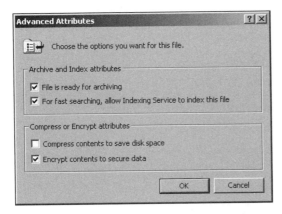

Figure 1-6   Advanced NTFS attributes for encrypting files and folders

12. Click **OK**.

13. Click **OK** a second time, and you will receive the message shown in Figure 1-7.

Figure 1-7   A warning given after files have been marked for encryption

14. Click the radio button that says **Encrypt the file only**.

15. Click **OK**.

16. Log off as Administrator and log on as User1.

17. Try to access the New Text Document in e:\Encryption\User2Folder. Access should be denied, even though the NTFS permissions are Everyone, Full Control.

18. Log off User1.

Certification Objectives

Objectives for CompTIA Security + Exam:

➤ General Security Concepts: Access Control

Review Questions

1. The best way to define encryption is:

   a. data that has not been tampered with intentionally or accidentally

   b. data that has been scrambled for remote transmission

   c. data that is secured so only the intended people have access

   d. data that can be accessed when it is needed

2. In Windows 2000 who can access encrypted files?

   a. The owner of the files

   b. The Administrator

   c. The Recovery Agent

   d. All users

3. If data that is encrypted with NTFS encryption is copied to a FAT partition, the data is decrypted. True or False?

4. What is the Windows 2000 command line utility that can be used to encrypt data?

   a. Crypto

   b. EncryptIt

   c. Encrypt

   d. Cipher

5. You have decided to use NTFS encryption to enhance security on your network of six servers. Five of the six servers have compressed drives, and a new administrator says that it would not be a good idea to implement an encryption policy at this time. Why is or isn't the administrator correct?

   a. The Administrator is not correct; encryption will help secure your network.

   b. The Administrator is not correct; encryption will decrease the performance of the servers, but it will not be noticeable to the users.

   c. The Administrator is correct; encryption would add too much overhead to the servers.

   d. The Administrator is correct; encryption and compression cannot be used at the same time.

CHAPTER TWO

AUTHENTICATION

2

Labs included in this chapter:

➤ Lab 2.1 Using the Windows 2000 Local Password Policy Settings for Length

➤ Lab 2.2 Using the Windows 2000 Local Password Policy Settings for Complexity

➤ Lab 2.3 Preventing the Display of the Last Logon Name

➤ Lab 2.4 Setting an Account Lockout Policy

➤ Lab 2.5 Using the RunAs Command to Bypass Security

CompTIA Security+ Exam Objectives	
Objective	Lab
General Security Concepts: Authentication	2.1, 2.2, 2.3, 2.4, 2.5
General Security Concepts: Authentication: Username/Password	2.1, 2.2

LAB 2.1 USING THE WINDOWS 2000 LOCAL PASSWORD POLICY SETTINGS FOR LENGTH

Objectives

Authentication is the process of verifying the identity of a person for the purposes of accessing information on a computer system. For authentication to work properly in a networking environment, a username and password are required. Unfortunately, most people take authentication lightly and do not follow basic security principles. They share passwords with others and sometimes even write them down. Enforcing security policies can be very difficult to manage, especially for large companies. Another problem with authentication is the length of passwords; short passwords or blank passwords are easier to crack. With this in mind, Windows 2000 has instituted a local password policy to allow you to specify the minimum length for passwords.

After completing this lab, you will be able to:

➤ Modify the Windows 2000 local security policy

➤ Change the **Minimum password length** password policy

Materials Required

This lab will require the following:

➤ A Windows 2000 server configured as a standalone server

➤ Administrator access to the server

➤ Two user-level accounts: User1 and User2. Each account should have the password "password" set up to access the account.

Estimated completion time: **10–15 minutes**

ACTIVITY

1. Log on to the Windows 2000 server as Administrator.

2. Click **Start**, **Programs**, **Administrative Tools**, then click **Local Security Policy**.

3. Expand **Account Policies**.

4. Click **Password Policy**. You will see a screen that resembles Figure 2-1.

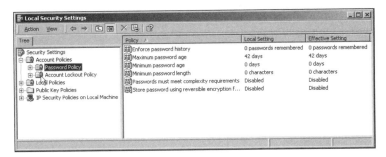

Figure 2-1   Local Security Settings default password policy

5. Double-click **Minimum password length**.

6. Change the characters value from **0** to **9**, as shown in Figure 2-2. (*Note:* The current password for the user accounts is "password." This will verify that the change worked.)

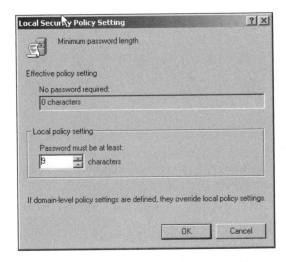

Figure 2-2   Password Length changed to nine characters

7. Click **OK**.

8. Close all windows and log off.

9. Log on as User1; Windows will allow you to use the existing password.

10. Press **Ctrl-Alt-Delete**.

11. Click **Change password…**.

12. Type **password** for the old password.

13. Type in a new password that is less than 9 characters in length in both the New Password and Confirm Password text boxes. This step is not meant to be successful.

This worked - reset to 8 to allow ~~uniquely~~ Reuwijo password

14. You will receive the following message: "Your password must be at least 9 characters and cannot repeat any of your previous 0 passwords. Please type a different password. Type a password which meets these requirements in both text boxes."

15. Try assigning **password1** as the new password. The password change will be successful.

Certification Objectives

Objectives for CompTIA Security+ Exam:

➤ General Security Concepts: Authentication: Username/Password

Review Questions

1. Which of the following best describes authentication?

   a. The process of gaining access to resources

   b. The process of utilizing resources

   c. The process of verifying the identification of a user

   d. The process of assigning permissions to users

2. Which of the following is required to authenticate to a Windows 2000 system? (Choose all that apply.)

   a. domain or computer name

   b. username

   c. PIN

   d. password

3. Why is password length important?

   a. Longer passwords are impossible to hack.

   b. Longer passwords are harder to hack.

   c. Windows requires long passwords in a domain environment.

   d. Longer passwords can prevent password cracking programs from working properly.

4. What is the recommended password length for Windows computers by most security professionals?

   a. six characters

   b. five characters

   c. eight characters

   d. seven characters

5. What is the reasoning behind the Windows password length recommendation?

   a. Windows hashes passwords.

   b. Users are less likely to write down a longer password.

   c. Windows crashes passwords.

   d. Windows uses Kerberos for passwords.

LAB 2.2 USING THE WINDOWS 2000 LOCAL PASSWORD POLICY SETTINGS FOR COMPLEXITY

Objectives

While the length of a password is very important, the complexity of a password is just as important. For example, a password that uses consecutive digits, such as 1234567 or abcdefg are not very secure, as a password cracking program could crack them in a short amount of time. With the Windows 2000 password complexity policy, a user is required to use at least three of the following: one number, one uppercase letter, one lowercase letter, or one symbol. Combining password length with complexity is a recommended method of most security professionals.

After completing this lab, you will be able to:

➤ Modify the Windows 2000 local security policy

➤ Change the **Passwords must meet complexity requirements** password policy

Materials Required

This lab will require the following:

➤ A Windows 2000 server configured as a standalone server

➤ Administrator access to the server

➤ Two user-level accounts: User1 and User2

Estimated completion time: **10–15 minutes**

ACTIVITY

1. Log on to the Windows 2000 server as Administrator.

2. Click **Start**, **Programs**, **Administrative Tools**, then click **Local Security Policy**.

3. Expand **Account Policies**.

4. Click **Password Policy**.

5. Double-click **Passwords must meet complexity requirements**.

6. Click the **Enabled** radio button, as shown in Figure 2-3.

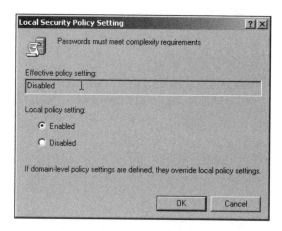

Figure 2-3   Password Complexity enabled

7. Click **OK**.

8. Close all windows and log off.

9. Log on as User1; Windows remembers that the password is set as password1.

10. Press **Ctrl-Alt-Delete**.

11. Click **Change password…**.

12. Type **password1** for the old password.

13. Type in **password** for the new password. Click **OK**.

14. You will receive the following message: "Your password must be at least 9 characters and cannot repeat any of your previous 0 passwords; must contain capitals, numerals or punctuation; and cannot contain your account or full name. Please type a different password. Type a password which meets these requirements in both text boxes."

15. Try assigning **Password1** as the new password. The password change will be successful. (*Note*: the old password is password1.)

Certification Objectives

Objectives for CompTIA Security+ Exam:

➤ General Security Concepts: Authentication: Username/Password

2

Review Questions

1. Why are complex passwords important? (Choose all that apply.)

    a. Complex passwords are more difficult to crack.

    b. The complexity of passwords add to the security of long passwords.

    c. Complex passwords are impossible to crack.

    d. Complex passwords help users create strong passwords.

2. Which of the following is considered a complex password? (Choose all that apply.)

    a. @1c4htj3

    b. Pa$$w0rd

    c. ncdjszkjdnc

    d. Ajd649sg

3. Even though you have implemented the recommended password length and complexity policy, applications such as ftp and telnet are not recommended for remote connections for which of the following reasons?

    a. Ftp and telnet require Kerberos.

    b. Ftp and telnet cannot use special characters in passwords.

    c. Ftp and telnet send passwords in plain text.

    d. Ftp and telnet have security exploits.

4. Which authentication protocol(s) that can encrypt passwords can be used with Windows 2000? (Choose all that apply.)

    a. CHAP

    b. PAP

    c. SPAP

    d. EAP

5. Which of the following is a remote access authentication protocol? (Choose all that apply.)

    a. CHAP

    b. MS-CHAP

    c. PAP

    d. SPA

LAB 2.3 PREVENTING THE DISPLAY OF THE LAST LOGON NAME

Objectives

One way to discourage a password hacker is to remove the name of the last user to logon from the Log On to Windows entry window. Without an account name, the hacker will have an extra step to complete before gaining access to the system. Otherwise, the hacker will know at least one account on the system and will have only to attempt to crack the password. This is especially useful on remote access computers. If someone has physical access to a computer, cracking passwords can be relatively easy.

After completing this lab, you will be able to:

➤ Modify the Windows 2000 local security policy

➤ Change the **Do not display last user name in logon screen** security option

Materials Required

This lab will require the following:

➤ A Windows 2000 server configured as a standalone server

➤ Administrator access to the server

➤ Two user-level accounts: User1 and User2

Estimated completion time: **10 minutes**

ACTIVITY

1. Log on to the Windows 2000 server as Administrator.

2. Click **Start**, **Programs**, **Administrative Tools**, then click **Local Security Policy**.

3. Expand **Local Policies**.

4. Click **Security Options**. A screen resembling Figure 2-4 will appear.

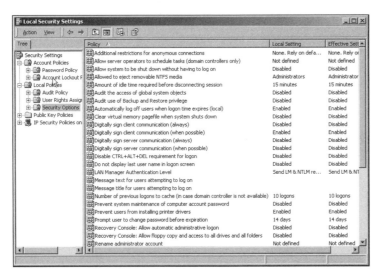

Figure 2-4   Local Security Settings default Security Options

5. Double-click **Do not display last user name in logon screen**.

6. Click the **Enable** radio button, as shown in Figure 2-5.

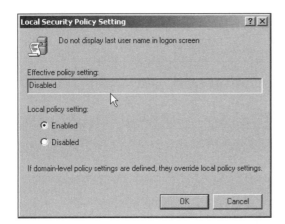

Figure 2-5   Do not display last user name in logon screen enabled

7. Click **OK**.

8. Close all windows and log off.

9. Press **Ctrl-Alt-Delete**.

10. Notice that the User name field is empty in the logon screen.

Certification Objectives

Objectives for CompTIA Security+ Exam:

➤ General Security Concepts: Authentication

Review Questions

1. What is the advantage in removing the name of the last user to log on?

    a. allows users to share computers

    b. requires users to remember their usernames

    c. requires a hacker to take an extra step when cracking passwords

    d. hides the identity of the Windows Domain

2. Which default Windows NT/2000 account should be renamed to assist this method of authentication protection?

    a. Domain Admins

    b. Domain Guests

    c. Administrator

    d. Guest

3. Which account should be disabled to assist this method of authentication protection?

    a. Guest

    b. Administrator

    c. User1

    d. User2

4. Who can delete the Guest Account?

    a. No one

    b. Administrator

    c. Domain Admins

    d. Guest

5. Biometrics is an additional method that can be used to secure authentication. Which of the following is an example of a biometric? (Choose all that apply.)

    a. complex passwords

    b. fingerprints

    c. retinal scans

    d. smart cards

LAB 2.4 SETTING AN ACCOUNT LOCKOUT POLICY

2

Objectives

Another measure that can be taken to create a roadblock for the hacker is to implement an account lockout policy. If a hacker has the time and patience, he or she can crack any password. An account lockout policy will disable an account for a specific amount of time after a certain number of failed logon attempts. This can help delay a successful hack attempt or better yet, discourage the hacker from continuing.

After completing this lab, you will be able to:

➤ Modify the Windows 2000 local security policy

➤ Change the **Account lockout threshold** account lockout policy

➤ Change the **Reset account lockout counter** account lockout policy

Materials Required

This lab will require the following:

➤ A Windows 2000 server configured as a standalone server

➤ Administrator access to the server

➤ Two user-level accounts: User1 and User2

Estimated completion time: **10–15 minutes**

ACTIVITY

1. Log on to the Windows 2000 server as Administrator.

2. Click **Start**, **Programs**, **Administrative Tools**, then click **Local Security Policy**.

3. Expand **Account Policies**.

4. Click **Account Lockout Policy**. A screen resembling Figure 2-6 will appear.

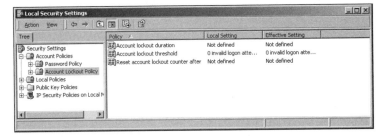

Figure 2-6   Default Account Lockout Policy

5. Double-click **Account lockout threshold**.

6. Change the invalid logon attempts to **3**, as shown in Figure 2-7.

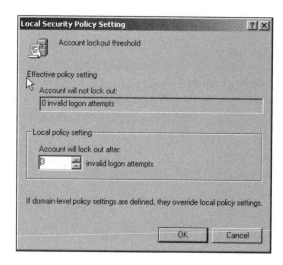

Figure 2-7   Changing the Account Lockout policy set to three invalid logon attempts

7. Click **OK**.

8. You will be prompted to change the values for the **Account lockout duration** and **Reset account lockout counter after** policies, as shown in Figure 2-8.

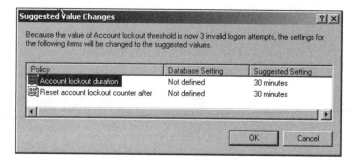

Figure 2-8   Suggested value changes for the Account Lockout Policy

9. Click **OK** to accept the changes and notice how the Local Setting changed, as shown in Figure 2-9.

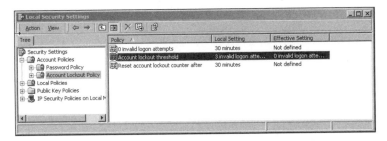

Figure 2-9   Account Lockout Policy Threshold is set to three attempts

10. Close all windows and log off.

11. Log on as User2 to verify the account is functional.

12. Log off User2 and try to log on three times without entering a password.

13. Try to log on a fourth time and you will receive the following message: **Unable to log you on because your account has been locked out, please contact your administrator.**

14. Click **OK**.

15. You can now either wait 30 minutes, or log on as Administrator and unlock the account, as shown in Figure 2-10, by right-clicking on the user account in the Local Users and Groups extension of the Computer Management snap-in under Administrative Tools.

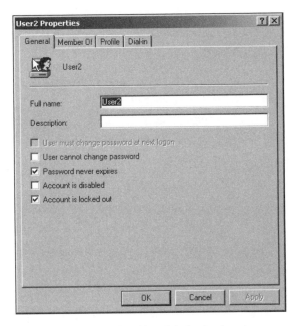

Figure 2-10   Notice User2 is locked out

Certification Objectives

Objectives for CompTIA Security+ Exam:

➤ General Security Concepts: Authentication

Review Questions

1. Why is it important to implement an account lockout policy?

   a. prevents users from forgetting passwords

   b. prevents hackers from hacking continuously

   c. forces users to write down passwords

   d. creates a log of hack attempts

2. Which settings can be configured in the Windows 2000 Account Lockout Policy? (Choose all that apply.)

   a. account lockout threshold

   b. account lockout duration

   c. account lockout length

   d. reset account lockout counter after

3. Which feature of the account lockout policy can be used to assist account operators when handling locked out accounts?

   a. account lockout threshold

   b. account lockout duration

   c. account lockout length

   d. reset account lockout counter after

4. How can an administrator access a system once the Administrator account has been locked out and a reset counter has not been set?

   a. Restore the account database from a backup.

   b. The Administrator account cannot be locked out.

   c. Reboot the computer.

   d. The system will be inaccessible.

5. If you implement an account lockout and reset counter policy, how can you monitor the failed attempts? (Choose all that apply.)

   a. Enable Account Policies.

   b. Check the System Log in the Event Viewer.

   c. Enable Auditing.

   d. Check the Security Log in the Event Viewer.

LAB 2.5 USING THE RUNAS COMMAND TO BYPASS SECURITY

2

Objectives

Before the explosion of e-mail viruses, many network administrators would use their administrative account to complete daily tasks such as composing memos and checking e-mail. After the "I Love You" virus was released and wreaked havoc on numerous network files, most companies required administrators to use two accounts. One account was for administrative tasks, and the other was for day-to-day tasks. While this practice is more secure, it is very inconvenient. Many administrators did what they could to find ways around this policy, including ignoring it. Windows 2000 has a new feature, the RunAs command, which fixes this problem. RunAs allows an administrator to log on with a standard user account and still run administrative programs with administrative rights. Those rights are only applied to the application, so viruses, worms, and Trojan Horses cannot access the network with administrative privileges.

After completing this lab, you will be able to:

➤ Identify RunAs procedures

➤ Run programs as Administrator, while logged on as a regular user.

Materials Required

This lab will require the following:

➤ A Windows 2000 server configured as a standalone server

➤ Administrator access to the server

➤ Two user-level accounts: User1 and User2

Estimated completion time: **10–15 minutes**

ACTIVITY

1. Log on as User2.

2. Try to open the **Local Security Policy**.

3. You will receive the error message shown in Figure 2-11.

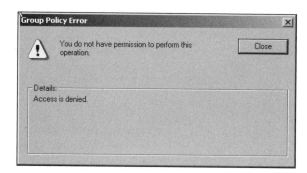

Figure 2-11   Users do not have permissions to access the Local Security Policy

4. Click **Close**.

5. Hold the **Shift** key down.

6. Right-click on the **Local Security Policy** icon.

7. Click **Run As**.

8. Enter the necessary Administrator account information, an example of which is shown in Figure 2-12.

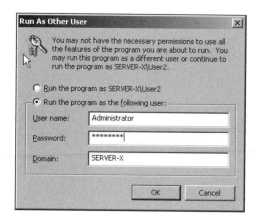

Figure 2-12   Using the RunAs command to access the Local Security Policy

9. Click **OK**.

10. You can now edit the Local Security Policy.

Certification Objectives

Objectives for CompTIA Security+ Exam:

➤ General Security Concepts: Authentication

Review Questions

1. Which of the following is an advantage in using the RunAs command?

   a. allows users to bypass security without permission

   b. helps prevent the spread of viruses

   c. conserves resources for administrators

   d. allows administrators to check e-mail and administer the network

2. Which of the following is a disadvantage of the RunAs command? (Choose all that apply.)

   a. opens potential security holes

   b. allows users to install applications if they know the local administrator password

   c. allows users to access administrative tools if they know the local administrator password

   d. allows users to change account permissions

3. How can you use RunAs on an existing shortcut?

   a. Hold down the Alt key and right-click the shortcut.

   b. Right-click the shortcut.

   c. Hold down the Shift key and right-click the shortcut.

   d. Hold down the Ctrl key and right-click the shortcut.

4. What application should you not use RunAs to execute?

   a. a virus scanner

   b. an e-mail application

   c. a word processor

   d. an auditing program

5. How can you prevent users from using RunAs?

   a. Delete the RunAs command.

   b. Disable the RunAs Service.

   c. Disable the Server Service.

   d. Delete the RunAs.dll file.

CHAPTER THREE

ATTACKS AND MALICIOUS CODE

Labs included in this chapter:

➤ Lab 3.1 Using the AT Command to Start System Processes

➤ Lab 3.2 Researching DOS and DDOS Attacks

➤ Lab 3.3 Researching the CPUHOG DOS Attack

➤ Lab 3.4 Researching the NetBus Trojan Horse

➤ Lab 3.5 Removing NetBus from an Infected System

CompTIA Security+ Exam Objectives	
Objective	Lab
General Security Concepts: Attacks: DOS/DDOS	3.2, 3.3
General Security Concepts: Malicious Code: Trojan Horses	3.1, 3.4, 3.5

LAB 3.1 USING THE AT COMMAND TO START SYSTEM PROCESSES

Objectives

One shortcoming of the Windows operating system is that it lacks the ability to execute a program on a remote system. If you connect to a server and double-click an executable, it runs on your system. There are Windows 2000 Resource Kit utilities available to assist with this, but there is another method that works well. Using the "at" command, you can schedule an executable to run on a remote system at a specific time. This is a common method used to install Trojan Horses.

After completing this lab, you will be able to:

➤ Use the at command to execute remote programs

➤ Find individual system processes and stop them

Materials Required

This lab will require the following:

➤ Two Windows 2000 servers to work in groups of two

➤ Administrator access to both servers

Estimated completion time: **30 minutes**

ACTIVITY

1. On Server-X, log in as Administrator.

2. Press **[Control]–[Alt]–[Delete]**.

3. Click **Task Manager**.

4. Click the **Processes** tab and make a note of the current processes. Hint: Look for notepad.exe. You should not see it.

5. On Server-Y, log in as Administrator.

6. Click **Start**, **Run**, and type **cmd**. Press **Enter**.

7. At the command line type **net time \\server-x** and then press **Enter**. This will tell you the current time for Server-Y so you can schedule the execution of a program.

Note: Server-X should be your partner's server name, Server-Y should be your server name, and the time should be the current time.

8. At the command line type **at \\server-x 3:49p /interactive "notepad.exe"** and then press **Enter**.

9. These steps are illustrated in Figure 3-1.

Figure 3-1   Using Net Time and the at command to schedule programs on a remote computer

10. At 3:49 P.M. notepad will launch on Server -X.

11. If you would like to launch a process that is hidden from your partner, repeat step 6 but remove the "/interactive" switch, as follows: **at \\server-x 3:49p "notepad.exe"**.

12. Once the time specified (3:49 P.M. in our example) has past, press **[Control]-[Alt]-[Delete]**.

13. Click **Task Manager**.

14. Click the **Processes** tab and look for **notepad.exe**, as in Figure 3-2. Note: The application was executed but did not appear on the screen. This is important for the next few labs when you will install Trojan Horses. To cause a program to launch you can use the /interactive switch for the at command.

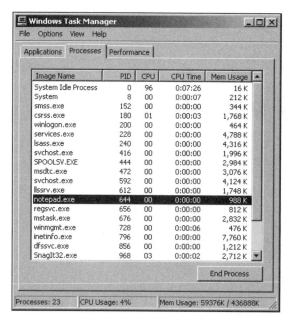

Figure 3-2   The Task Manager showing the Notepad.exe process running

Certification Objectives

Objectives for CompTIA Security+ Exam:

➤ General Security Concepts: Malicious Code: Trojan Horses

REVIEW QUESTIONS

1. Which of the following best describes the "at" command?

   a. a program that can execute commands and programs needed to install program updates

   b. a program that can schedule commands and programs to run on a computer at a specific time and date

   c. a Resource Kit Utility that can schedule commands and programs to run on a computer at a specific time and date

   d. a Trojan Horse that can schedule commands and programs to run on a computer at a specific time and date

2. What switch will allow the user to see the process that was started with the "at" command?

   a. /delete

   b. /interaction

   c. /interactive

   d. /visible

3. Which of the following is a legitimate use for "at"?

   a. scheduling backups

   b. scheduling virus scans

   c. scheduling updates

   d. all of the above

4. What is the result of the following command: at \\server-x 3:25 "notepad"?

   a. A notepad process will launch on server-x immediately.

   b. A notepad process will launch on server-x at 3:25 P.M.

   c. A notepad process will launch on server-x at 3:25 A.M.

   d. Nothing, the command was incorrectly entered.

5. What is the result of the following command: at \\server-y 14 /delete?

   a. Scheduled id 14 will be deleted from the schedule on server-y.

   b. Scheduled id 14 will be deleted from the schedule on server-x.

   c. Scheduled id 14 will be added to the schedule on server-x.

   d. Scheduled id 14 will be deleted from the schedule on the local system.

LAB 3.2 RESEARCHING DOS AND DDOS ATTACKS

Objectives

Hackers are not always interested in gaining access to resources and stealing information. Sometimes they just want to entertain themselves by preventing a company from doing business online. This is called a Denial of Service attack, or DOS. There are many ways to cause a DOS, but the general idea is to overload a system so that it cannot respond to legitimate customers. One of TCP/IP's useful utilities, ping, can be used in a malicious way to cause a DOS. If you ping a system with an IP address, it will reply. The idea behind using the ping utility to cause a DOS attack is to bombard a system with ICMP packets (used by ping) so that it cannot respond to legitimate requests. In this case, it may take what is called a Distributed DOS (DDOS), in which multiple machines work together to perform the attack.

After completing this lab, you will be able to:

➤ Understand how a DOS attack works

➤ Know how to prevent and respond to a DOS attack

Materials Required

This lab will require the following:

➤ A Windows 2000 server with Internet access

Estimated completion time: **30 minutes**

www.cisco.com/warp/ public/ 707/newStart.html

ACTIVITY

1. Search the Internet for "Denial of Service" and "Distributed Denial of Service". A comprehensive description can be found on the CERT Coordination Center Web site located at the following URL: *www.cert.org/tech_tips/denial_of_service.html*.

2. List five applications that perform a denial of service or distributed denial of service.

3. Find the origin of the application.

4. Are the DOS and DDOS attacks common types of attacks?

5. Describe the effects of a DOS or DDOS attack.

Certification Objectives

Objectives for CompTIA Security+ Exam:

➤ General Security Concepts: Attacks: DOS/DDOS

Review Questions

1. What does the acronym ICMP stand for?
   a. Internet Computer Management Protocol
   b. Internet Control Management Protocol
   c. Internet Control Message Protocol
   d. Internet Computer Message Protocol

2. Which of the following is a program that uses ICMP?
   a. DNS
   b. ftp
   c. telnet
   d. ping

3. What kind of attack uses multiple computers to attack another computer?
   a. Denial of Service
   b. Denial of System
   c. Distributed Denial of System
   d. Distributed Denial of Service

3

4. Which of the following sends packets to a destination but never completes the third step of the TCP handshake?

   a. DOS

   b. SYN Attack

   c. SYN Flood

   d. SYN Flop

5. A hacker modifies the source address of a packet so it appears to be a different host. This is known as which of the following?

   a. spoofing

   b. faking

   c. spooling

   d. masking

LAB 3.3 RESEARCHING THE CPUHOG DOS ATTACK

Objectives

The three most important resources for a computer are memory, storage, and processor power. If you take any one of the three away, the system is useless. In this lab, you will use a program called CPUHOG, which will consume most of the processor's resources and cause a DOS. CPUHOG accomplishes this by setting its process priority level to the highest level possible, which is 16. Windows will try to fix this problem, but it only increases an application's priority to 15. As you may guess, CPUHOG will always have priority over other applications, including Task Manager. This could require a cold boot to restore the system's functionality.

After completing this lab, you will be able to:

➤ Understand processor resources and priority

➤ Describe the impact CPUHOG can have on a system

Materials Required

This lab will require the following:

➤ A Windows 2000 server with Internet access

Estimated completion time: **30 minutes**

ACTIVITY

1. Search the Internet for "CPUHOG".

2. Write a short summary describing a CPUHOG.

3. Search the Internet for "Windows application priorities".

4. Write a short summary explaining Windows System application and process priorities.

5. Describe the impact CPUHOG would have on your server if you were attacked with it.

Certification Objectives

Objectives for CompTIA Security+ Exam:

➤ General Security Concepts: Attacks: DOS/DDOS

REVIEW QUESTIONS

1. Which of the following is the most important computer resource?

   a. processor

   b. disk space

   c. memory

   d. all of the above

2. How many priority levels are available in Windows?

   a. 1

   b. 32

   c. 16

   d. 15

3. What is the highest priority that Windows will give applications?

   a. 1

   b. 32

   c. 16

   d. 15

4. What best describes CPUHOG?

   a. a program that consumes most of the processor's resources

   b. a program that consumes most of the memory's resources

   c. a program that consumes most of the hard drive's resources

   d. a program that consumes most of the computer's resources

5. The reason CPUHOG is successful in its DOS is because Windows allows applications to set their own priority. True or False?

Lab 3.4 Researching the NetBus Trojan Horse

Objectives

Another goal of a hacker is to gain access to a system without the user's knowledge. Programs that can allow this type of access are called Trojan Horses. A Trojan Horse is a program that may seem to be desirable, but it is actually harmful. One of the most well-known Trojan Horses is NetBus. NetBus was originally created in 1998 as a remote administration tool, with some additional tools with which to have fun. These tools could be used to redirect ports, launch applications, and even view the screen of a remote user. NetBus was distributed to some unsuspecting users with a game called Whack-a-Mole, then officially becoming a Trojan Horse. The users thought they had a fun game to play, but it was actually a harmful program. Because Whack-a-Mole was fun, the users also forwarded the game to all of their friends. Today, most virus detection software will prevent NetBus from successfully attacking a system.

After completing this lab, you will be able to:

➤ Understand the impact Trojan Horses have on networks

➤ Describe the origins and effects of the NetBus Trojan Horse.

Materials Required

This lab will require the following:

➤ A Windows 2000 server with Internet access

Estimated completion time: **30 minutes**

Activity

1. Search the Internet for "NetBus Trojan Horse".

2. Write a one-page summary of the history of NetBus.

3. List the different versions and the features associated with each version of NetBus.

4. Explain the difference between the client and server components of NetBus.

5. Describe the effects of the NetBus Trojan Horse.

Certification Objectives

Objectives for CompTIA Security+ Exam:

➤ General Security Concepts: Malicious Code: Trojan Horses

Review Questions

1. Which of the following best describes a Trojan Horse?

    a. a program that requires a host program to run

  • b. a program that does something other than it appears to be intended to do

    c. a program that contains a mistake in the programming code

    d. a self-contained program that can replicate itself

2. Which of the following applications can help in preventing the spread of Trojan Horses? (Choose all that apply.)

  ~ a. firewall

  • b. virus scanner

    c. program debugger

    d. router

3. Which of the following ports is commonly associated with NetBus?

    a. 31337

    b. 65000

    c. 1024

    d. 12345

4. Which of the following are components of NetBus? (Choose all that apply.)

    a. dynamic libraries

    b. directory

    c. client

    d. server

5. Which of the following can NetBus accomplish? (Choose all that apply.)

    a. switch mouse buttons

    b. launch applications

    c. capture screens

    d. redirect ports

LAB 3.5 REMOVING NETBUS FROM AN INFECTED SYSTEM

Objectives

The following lab can be useful if you have been infected with the NetBus Trojan Horse. All recent virus detection software can prevent NetBus from attacking a system, but they do not do a good job of removing it. With each release of NetBus, it became more difficult to remove. This lab contains all of the necessary steps to remove NetBus 1.7. If you

3

are not infected, this lab can be a good tool for your network security toolbox. You should also research on the Internet how to remove other versions of this Trojan Horse.

After completing this lab, you will be able to:

➤ Determine if NetBus is installed on a system

➤ Remove NetBus from a system and prevent future attacks.

Materials Required

This lab will require the following:

➤ A Windows 2000 server

➤ Administrator access to the server

➤ A PC infected with the NetBus Trojan Horse (Optional)

Estimated completion time: **15–30 minutes**

ACTIVITY

The servers used in this activity will be referred to as Server-X and Server-Y. Please substitute the names of your servers for these names.

1. Log on to server-y as Administrator.

2. Click **Start**, **Search**, **For Files or Folders**. Note: Some of the files listed in steps 2-7 may not exist.

3. Search for **patch.exe** and delete any results.

4. Search for **rundll.dll** and delete any results. Note: Do not delete rundll32.exe.

5. Search for **keyhook.dl_** and delete any results.

6. Search for **keyhook.dll** and delete any results.

7. Search for **nbsetup1.reg** and delete any results.

8. Search for **nbsetup2.reg** and delete any results.

9. Close the Search Window.

10. Click **Start**, **Run**, **Regedit** and then press **Enter**.

11. Navigate to **HKEY_LOCAL_MACHINE\SOFTWARE\Microsoft\ Windows\CurrentVersion\Run**.

12. Delete the key name: **PATCH. The value of the key should be C:\WINNT\patch.exe /nomsg"**. Note: It is possible for NetBus to use a different name than patch.exe, but it will always end with /nomsg. This screen is shown in Figure 3-3 below.

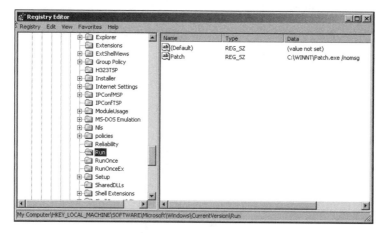

Figure 3-3   Patch.exe is the client program that NetBus adds to the registry

13. Navigate to **HKEY_LOCAL_MACHINE\SOFTWARE\Microsoft\ Windows\CurrentVersion\RunServices**.

14. Delete the keys referring to **rundll** and **rundll32** if they exist.

15. Reboot the computer and NetBus will be gone. At this point you should check the "at" schedule and install a virus program to protect the system.

Certification Objectives

Objectives for CompTIA Security+ Exam:

➤ General Security Concepts: Malicious Code: Trojan Horses

REVIEW QUESTIONS

1. Which version of NetBus allows the default port to be changed?

   a. 1.20

   b. 1.50

   c. 1.60

   d. 1.70

2. Which Trojan Horse is similar to NetBus?

   a. BackOffice

   b. BackOrifice

   c. BackBacon

   d. BackUps

3. Which of the following are games known to be associated to NetBus? (Choose all that apply.)

   a. Hack–a–Mole

   b. Whack–a–Mole

   c. Whackjob

   d. Whackmole

4. The removal process for NetBus is different depending on the version. True or False?

5. Which of the following files is the Client portion of NetBus?

   a. netBus.exe

   b. patch.exe

   c. packs.exe

   d. rundll32.exe

3

CHAPTER FOUR

REMOTE ACCESS

Labs included in this chapter:

➤ Lab 4.1 Enabling Dial-in Access

➤ Lab 4.2 Configuring a Windows 2000 VPN Server

➤ Lab 4.3 Using PPTP to Connect to a VPN Server

➤ Lab 4.4 Attempting to Use L2TP to Connect to a VPN Server

➤ Lab 4.5 Configuring a Remote Access Policy

CompTIA Security+ Exam Objectives	
Objective	Lab
Communication Security: Remote Access: VPN	4.1, 4.2, 4.3, 4.4, 4.5
Communication Security: Remote Access: L2TP/PPTP	4.3, 4.4
Communication Security: Remote Access: Vulnerabilities	4.5

LAB 4.1 ENABLING DIAL-IN ACCESS

Objectives

Remote access to a network is an essential utility for Administrators and remote users. Without it, Administrators would have to remain in a computer room to do their tasks, and remote users would have to use "snail mail" or fax machines to transfer data. Windows NT/2000 allows remote access, but, by default, Windows NT/2000 does not allow dial-in access. Dial-in access includes more than modem access; it also includes VPN access.

After completing this lab, you will be able to:

➤ Edit user properties to grant users dial-in access

➤ Edit user properties to remove dial-in access

Materials Required

This lab will require the following:

➤ A Windows 2000 standalone server

➤ Administrator access to the server

➤ Two accounts, User1 and User2, with Administrator access

Estimated completion time: **10 minutes**

ACTIVITY

1. Log on as Administrator.

2. Right-click **My Computer** and select **Manage**.

3. Expand **Local Users and Groups** and click **Users**.

4. Double-click **Administrator**.

5. Click the **Dial-in** tab.

6. Select the **Allow access** radio button, as shown in Figure 4-1.

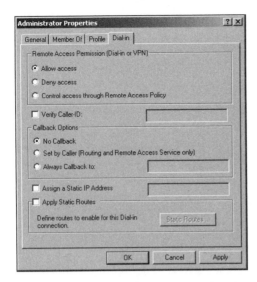

Figure 4-1 Allow remote access by changing the Dial-in Properties for user accounts

7. Click **OK**.

8. Log on as User1 and repeat steps 4–8. Do the same for User2.

9. Close the **Computer Management** window and log off.

Certification Objectives

Objectives for CompTIA Security+ Exam:

➤ Communication Security: Remote Access: VPN

Review Questions

1. Dial-in access is enabled for the Administrator account only. True or False?

2. Which administrative tool is used to allow dial-in access in a Windows NT environment?

   a. Active Directory users and computers

   b. user manager

   c. computer management

   d. server manager

3. Which administrative tool is used to allow dial-in access in a Windows 2000 Workgroup environment?

   a. Active Directory users and computers

   b. user manager

   c. computer management

   d. server manager

4. Which administrative tool is used to allow dial-in access in a Windows 2000 Domain environment?

   a. Active Directory users and computers

   b. user manager

   c. computer management

   d. server manager

5. When dial-in access is enabled, Terminal services access is also enabled. True or False?

LAB 4.2 CONFIGURING A WINDOWS 2000 VPN SERVER

Objectives

In the past, most companies set up modem pools that were connected to remote access servers to enable remote access for employees. This method worked, but had some short-comings. For example, modem pools required additional phone lines and support of the modems and phone lines. Given the relative unreliability of modems, this proved to be a problematic solution. Many companies used a third party to supply the phone lines and modems to avoid having to support the equipment. Virtual Private Networks (VPNs) can be used to replace modem pools and keep support internal, while also keeping over-head to a minimum. A VPN uses public Internet connections for private communica-tion. The information is kept confidential by using tunneling protocols, which you will learn about in the following labs.

After completing this lab, you will be able to:

➤ Use the Windows 2000 Routing and Remote Access Service

➤ Configure a Windows 2000 Server to accept VPN connections

Materials Required

This lab will require the following:

➤ Two Windows 2000 servers configured as standalone servers

➤ Administrator access to both servers

➤ Two user-level accounts: User1 and User2

Estimated completion time: **10–15 minutes**

ACTIVITY

The servers used in this activity will be referred to as Server-X and Server-Y. Please substitute the names of your servers for these names.

4

1. On Server-X, click **Start**, **Programs**, **Administrative Tools**, **Routing and Remote Access**.

2. Notice that the server has next to it an icon of a red arrow pointing down, as seen in Figure 4-2.

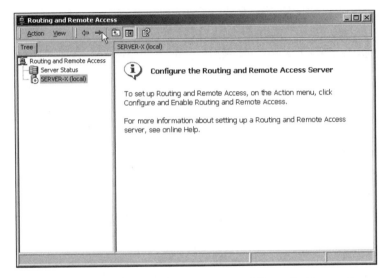

Figure 4-2   Configuring the Routing and Remote Access Server with the service stopped

3. To configure the server, right-click the server name.

4. Select **Configure and Enable Routing and Remote Access**.

5. The Routing and Remote Access Server Setup Wizard will begin.

6. Click **Next**.

7. Select the **Virtual Private Network (VPN) server** radio button.

8. Click **Next**.

9. Click **Next** at the Remote Client Protocols step to accept the default value of TCP/IP....

10. Click **Next** at the Internet Connection step to accept the default value of **<No internet connection>**.

11. Click **Next** at the Network Selection step, making sure that the appropriate network is selected. In this case you should choose the network that is accessible by the computers in use.

12. Click **Next** at the IP Address Assignment step. The **Automatically** option should work, as the Instructor server is providing DHCP services.

13. You will receive the message shown in Figure 4-3.

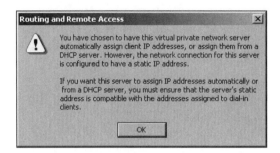

Figure 4-3   A DHCP warning message

14. Click **OK**.

15. Click **Next** at the Managing Multiple Remote Access Servers step. The default value of **No, I don't want to set up this server to use RADIUS now** should be selected.

16. Click **Finish**.

17. You will receive the message shown in Figure 4-4, notifying you that you will have to configure the DHCP Relay Agent with the IP address of the server providing DHCP.

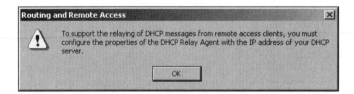

Figure 4-4   Warning message notifying you that the DHCP relay agent must know the IP address of the DHCP server

18. The Routing and Remote Access service will start.

19. Expand **IP Routing**.

20. Right-click **DHCP Relay Agent** and select **Properties**.

21. Enter the IP address of the Instructor's server. (You can obtain this information from your Instructor.)

22. Click **Add**, and then click **OK**.

23. Click **OK**.

24. Close the **Routing and Remote Access** window.

25. Log off Administrator.

Certification Objectives

Objectives for CompTIA Security+ Exam:

➤ Communication Security: Remote Access: VPN

Review Questions

1. Which of the following Windows Operating Systems support VPN connections? (Choose all that apply.)

   a. Windows NT

   b. Windows 2000

   c. Windows 98

   d. Windows 3.11

2. Which of the following Windows operating systems support L2TP?

   a. Windows NT

   b. Windows 2000

   c. Windows 98

   d. Windows 3.11

3. Which of the following Windows operating systems can run RRAS?

   a. Windows NT

   b. Windows 2000

   c. Windows 98

   d. Windows 3.11

4. Which of the following Windows operating systems can run a VPN server service? (Choose all that apply.)

   a. Windows NT

   b. Windows 2000

   c. Windows 98

   d. Windows 3.11

5. Remote Access policies can be configured with Windows 2000 Group Policy. True or False?

LAB 4.3 USING PPTP TO CONNECT TO A VPN SERVER

Objectives

Point to Point Protocol (PPP) is a remote access protocol that improves on the previous standard, Serial Line Interface Protocol (SLIP). SLIP, the first remote access protocol for TCP/IP, had some major drawbacks. With SLIP, only static IP addresses could be used, and it lacked error correction. PPP addresses all of these issues. Another protocol, PPTP, is a tunneling protocol that uses PPP for encryption. PPTP is the primary protocol used for VPN connections.

After completing this lab, you will be able to:

➤ Set up and enable a dial-up connection to a VPN server using PPTP

Materials Required

This lab will require the following:

➤ Two Windows 2000 servers configured as standalone servers

➤ One of the servers configured as a VPN server

➤ Administrator access to both servers

➤ Two user-level accounts: User1 and User2

Estimated completion time: **15–20 minutes**

ACTIVITY

This lab requires that two servers be used. Substitute the names of your servers for Server-X and Server-Y. Server-X signifies the server that should be configured to accept VPN connections.

1. On Server-Y, click **Start**, **Settings**, **Network and Dial-up Connections**.

2. Double-click **Make New Connection**. You may be prompted to enter **Location Information**. If so, enter your area code then click **OK** twice.

3. Click **Next** at the Network Connection Wizard.

4. Select **Connect to a private network through the Internet**.

5. Click **Next**.

6. Enter the host name of the VPN server (Server-X).

7. Click **Next** at the **Connection Availability** step, enabling the connection for all users.

8. Click **Next** at the **Internet connection Sharing** step. Do not enable Internet Connection Sharing.

9. You will be prompted to give the connection a name; call it **PPTP VPN**.

10. Check the box **Add a shortcut to my desktop**.

11. Click **Finish**.

12. You will automatically be prompted to log on.

13. Log on as Administrator. You are now connected.

14. To see what happens if an account does not have dial-in access, go to Server-X and disable dial-in access. Try to connect again.

15. Close all windows and log off.

Certification Objectives

Objectives for CompTIA Security+ Exam:

➤ Communication Security: Remote Access: VPN

➤ Communication Security: Remote Access: L2TP/PPTP

Review Questions

1. Which of the following is the PPTP control port?

   a. UDP 1723

   b. TCP 1723

   c. TCP 1494

   d. UDP 1494

2. What do the LCP extensions provide for PPTP?

   a. error correction for the data link connection

   b. Data Link layer tunneling

   c. establish, configure, and test the data link connection

   d. link and connect the PPTP connection

3. Which of the following protocols can be used with PPTP? (Choose all that apply.)

   a. IPX/SPX

   b. NetBEUI

   c. TCP/IP

   d. AppleTalk

4. Which protocol does PPTP use for encryption?

   a. PPP

   b. IPSec

   c. ESP

   d. PPTP can encrypt without another protocol.

5. Which of the following operating systems supports PPTP? (Choose all that apply.)

   a. Windows 2000

   b. Windows NT

   c. Windows 3.11

   d. Windows 9.x

LAB 4.4 ATTEMPTING TO USE L2TP TO CONNECT TO A VPN SERVER

Objectives

L2TP is another extension to the PPP protocol but merges the features of PPTP and Layer Two Forwarding (L2F). PPTP is a Microsoft protocol and L2F is a Cisco protocol. There are two main components of L2TP: L2TP Access Concentrator (LAC), which physically terminates a call, and L2TP Network Server (LNS), which terminates and authenticates the PPP stream. L2TP is a tunneling protocol that relies on another protocol to provide encryption. IPSec is commonly used with L2TP and provides encryption.

After completing this lab, you will be able to:

➤ Configure a VPN connection for use with the L2TP protocol

➤ Access a VPN server using the L2TP protocol

Materials Required

This lab will require the following:

➤ Two Windows 2000 servers configured as standalone servers

➤ Administrator access to both servers

➤ Two user-level accounts: User1 and User2

Estimated completion time: **15–20 minutes**

ACTIVITY

This lab requires that two servers be used. Substitute the names of your servers for Server-X and Server-Y. Server-X signifies the server that should be configured to accept VPN connections.

1. On Server-Y, click **Start**, **Settings**, **Network and Dial-up Connections**.

2. Double-click **Make New Connection**.

3. Click **Next** at the Network Connection Wizard.

4. Select **Connect to a private network through the Internet**.

5. Click **Next**.

6. Enter the host name of the VPN server (Server-X).

7. Click **Next** at the **Connection Availability** step, enabling the connection for all users.

8. Click **Next** at the **Internet Connection Sharing** step. Do not enable Internet Connection Sharing.

9. You will be prompted to give the connection a name, call it **L2TP VPN**.

10. Check the box **Add a shortcut to my desktop**.

11. Click **Finish**. You will automatically be prompted to log on.

12. Click **Properties**, and then click the **Networking** tab.

13. Under **Type of VPN server I am calling**, select Layer-2 Tunneling Protocol (L2TP), then click **OK**.

14. Enter the Administrator password and click **Connect**.

15. It will take a few seconds, but you will receive an error message that the connection requires a certificate and no certificate was found. You will then be disconnected. To use L2TP, a Certificate Authority is required. You will configure a Certificate Authority in a later chapter, at which time you can revisit this lab to test L2TP VPN connections.

16. Close all windows and log off.

Certification Objectives

Objectives for CompTIA Security+ Exam:

➤ Communication Security: Remote Access: VPN

➤ Communication Security: Remote Access: L2TP/PPTP

Review Questions

1. L2TP is compatible only with the TCP/IP protocol suite. True or False?

2. L2TP cannot provide encryption for transmission. True or False?

3. What layer of the OSI model does IPSec operate?

   a. Data Link

   b. Network

   c. Presentation

   d. Physical

4. Which of the following operating systems supports L2TP?

   a. Windows 2000

   b. Windows NT

   c. Windows 3.11

   d. Windows 9.x

5. L2TP over IPSec is not compatible with Network Address Translation. True or False?

Lab 4.5 Configuring a Remote Access Policy

Objectives

While remote access is an essential tool for today's businesses, it also has the potential to open a wide range of security holes. One way an administrator can overcome this is by using Windows 2000 Remote Access Policies. Remote Access Policies can lock down a remote access system to ensure that only those intended to have access are actually granted that access.

After completing this lab, you will be able to:

➤ Create a new Remote Access Policy

➤ Specify the time users can use the VPN connection

Materials Required

This lab will require the following:

➤ Two Windows 2000 servers configured as standalone servers

➤ Administrator access to both servers

➤ Two user-level accounts: User1 and User2

Estimated completion time: **15–20 minutes**

ACTIVITY

This lab requires two servers. Substitute the names of your servers for Server-X and Server-Y.

1. Log on to Server-X.

2. Load the **Routing and Remote Access** utility.

3. Right-click on **Remote Access Policies**.

4. Select **New Remote Access Policy**.

5. In the **Policy friendly name:** box, type **Allow All Users Access**.

6. Click **Next**.

7. Click the **Add** button to select an attribute.

8. Click **Day-And-Time-Restrictions**, then click **Add**.

9. Allow all hours.

10. Click **OK**.

11. Click **Next**.

12. Click the **Grant remote access permission** radio button.

13. Click **Next**.

14. Click **Finish**. Click **Remote Access Policies**, if necessary.

15. Right-click **Allow All Users Access** and select **Move up**.

16. In **Computer Management**, change the dial-in access for User1 and User2 to **Control access through Remote Access Policy**. *Note:* This option is only available in native mode.

17. Log on to Server-Y and try to access the PPTP VPN connection. You will be successful.

Certification Objectives

Objectives for CompTIA Security+ Exam:

➤ Communication Security: Remote Access: VPN

➤ Communication Security: Remote Access: Vulnerabilities

Review Questions

1. The default Remote Access Policy is to allow access if dial-in permission is enabled. True or False?

2. Which of the following is a Remote Access Policy attribute? (Choose all that apply.)

   a. Called–Station–ID

   b. Caller–Station–ID

   c. Client–IP–Address

   d. Tunnel–Type

3. Remote access logging can log which of the following events?

   a. accounting requests

   b. authentication requests

   c. periodic status

   d. all of the above

4. Which of the following can remote access servers provide to clients? (Choose all that apply.)

   a. DHCP

   b. IP spoofing

   c. DHCP relay

   d. DCHP repair

5. The default maximum port limit for each device that supports multiple ports is set to:

   a. 1

   b. 0

   c. 256

   d. 128

E-MAIL

Labs included in this chapter:

➤ Lab 5.1 Installing Hotmail and PGP and Configuring PGP Options

➤ Lab 5.2 Preventing PGP from Caching Your Passphrase

➤ Lab 5.3 Exporting Your Public Key

➤ Lab 5.4 Sending an Anonymous E-mail

➤ Lab 5.5 Creating a Hidden, Malicious File Attachment

CompTIA Security+ Exam Objectives	
Objective	**Lab**
Communication Security: Email	5.1, 5.2, 5.3, 5.4, 5.5
Communication Security: Email: PGP	5.1, 5.2
Communication Security: Email: Vulnerabilities	5.4, 5.5

LAB 5.1 INSTALLING HOTMAIL AND PGP AND CONFIGURING PGP OPTIONS

Objectives

The widespread use of the Internet and electronic mail opened a completely new way to communicate. Prior to e-mail, you would have to make a long distance telephone call to communicate with someone across the country or world. While telephone calls are still more personal, an e-mail can be edited, giving you the chance to more carefully craft your message. The risk involved with using e-mail, however, is that the medium used to send the e-mail messages is public, and therefore susceptible to network sniffing. One way to protect your information is to use Pretty Good Privacy (PGP) to sign and encrypt e-mail messages.

After completing this lab, you will be able to:

➤ Install Hotmail

➤ Install PGP

➤ Configure PGP to sign e-mail messages automatically

➤ Configure PGP to encrypt e-mail messages automatically

Materials Required

This lab will require the following:

➤ A Windows 2000 server with Microsoft Outlook Express installed

➤ A Hotmail account with PGP installed

➤ This lab should be completed with a partner who has the same materials.

Estimated completion time: **60 minutes**

ACTIVITY

To install and configure Hotmail:

1. Open your Web browser and navigate to *www. hotmail.com*.

2. Click the link for **Sign Up**.

3. Enter the registration information and click the button labeled **I Agree**, to accept the terms of the end-user license agreement.

4. After completing the registration process, navigate back to *www.hotmail.com*.

5. Verify that your account is active by entering your Sign-In Name and Password, then click **Sign In**.

6. Click the **Sign Out** button.

7. Launch **Outlook Express**.

8. Click the **Tools** menu and select **Accounts…**.

9. Click the **Mail** tab, then click the **Add** button and select **Mail…**.

10. Enter your name and click **Next**.

11. Enter your new e-mail address and click **Next**.

12. Select **HTTP server** and select **Hotmail** as your HTTP mail service provider, then click **Next**.

13. Verify that your Hotmail account name is listed correctly, then enter your password. Make sure the **Log on using Secure Password Authentication (SPA)** check box is selected, then click **Next**.

14. Click **Finish** to complete the process. Click **Close** in the Internet Accounts window, then click **No** in the Outlook Express window.

To download and install PGP:

1. Navigate to *www.pgpi.org/download* and download the flavor of PGP version 7 for your operating system.

2. Run the installation program and click **Next** to move past the initial screen.

3. Accept the licensing agreement and click **Yes**.

4. Click **Next** to skip the Read Me file for PGPfreeware.

5. The User Type screen asks if you want to use an existing PGP keyring. Since this will be a new installation of PGP for the purposes of this exercise, select **No, I'm a New User**, and click **Next**.

6. Choose an installation directory for PGP and click **Next**. The default directory is recommended.

7. On the Select Components screen, select the following:

   ■ **PGP Key Management**
   ■ **PGP Plugin for Microsoft Outlook Express**
   ■ **PGP Documentation**

   and then click **Next**.

8. On the Start Copying Files screen, you have the opportunity to review your selections before starting the installation. Click **Next**.

9. You may see an advertisement for the retail version of PGP. If so, simply click **Next**.

10. After all files have been copied to the installation directory, the PGPnet Set Adapter window will appear. Select **All Network and Dial-up Adapters** and click **OK**.

11. Click **Finish** to restart your computer.

To create PGP keys:

1. Launch Outlook Express.

2. Click **Tools**, **PGP**, **Launch PGPkeys**.

3. On the menu bar, click **Keys**, **New Key**.

4. Click **Next** to start the PGP Key Generation Wizard.

5. Enter your full name and e-mail address.

6. Click **Next**.

7. Enter a passphrase. A longer passphrase is desirable for security reasons.

8. Click **Next**. The key will be generated.

9. Click **Next**, then click **Finish**.

10. Close the **PGPkeys** window and do not save a backup.

To configure PGP:

1. Log in as Administrator. If necessary, click **Cancel** in the Key Generation Wizard window.

2. Launch **Outlook Express**.

3. On the Menu bar, click **Tools**, **PGP**, **Options....**

4. If necessary, click the **Email** tab.

5. Check the boxes **Encrypt new messages by default** and **Sign new messages by default**, as shown in Figure 5-1. (**Word wrap clear-signed messages** will be checked by default.)

6. Click **OK**.

7. Send a new message by clicking the **Send Mail** button.

8. Notice the **Encrypt Message (PGP)** and **Sign Message (PGP)** buttons are selected by default, as shown in Figure 5-2.

9. Enter your partner's e-mail address in the Address box.

10. Enter **Test Message** for the subject, and enter **Testing** in the body of the message.

11. Click the **Send Message** button, and you will be prompted to enter your Passphrase.

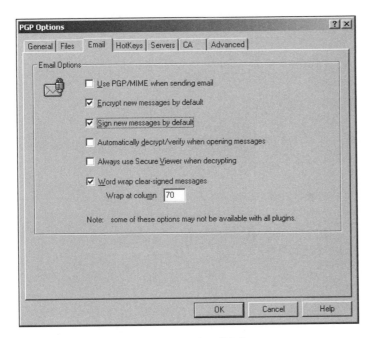

Figure 5-1   The PGP Options Email tab

Figure 5-2   A new e-mail message with the Encrypt Message (PGP) and Sign Message
options (PGP) enabled

12. Enter your Passphrase. Notice the **Hide Typing** box is checked, to prevent anyone from reading the text, as shown in Figure 5-3.

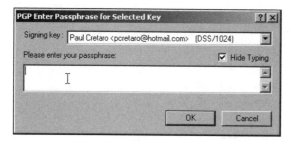

Figure 5-3 PGP passphrase entry window

13. Click **OK**. The message will be sent.

Certification Objectives

Objectives for CompTIA Security+ Exam:

➤ Communication Security: E-mail

➤ Communication Security: E-mail: PGP

Review Questions

1. E-mail is a susceptible intermediary modification because:

   a. it uses the Internet to transmit

   b. it is an open source application

   c. it sends messages in clear text

   d. it sends messages in cipher test

2. Which of the following are technologies used to send secure e-mail? (Choose all that apply.)

   a. PGP

   b. MIME

   c. S/MIME

   d. PCP

3. An alternative to using e-mail encryption would be to use:

   a. a Web browser

   b. a dial-in access method

   c. a virtual private network

   d. an ISDN connection

4. Which of the following are features of secure e-mail? (Choose all that apply.)

   a. authentication

   b. confidentiality

   c. integrity

d. non-repudiation

e. all of the above

5. Which of the following is a type of encryption? (Choose all that apply.)

a. conventional cryptography

b. traditional cryptography

c. public key cryptography

d. private key cryptography

5

Lab 5.2 Preventing PGP from Caching Your Passphrase

Objectives

PGP does an excellent job in verifying the source of an e-mail and encrypting the contents. Part of this process is entering a passphrase to gain access to your key. If someone can gain access to your PC, however, they may be able to impersonate you by using a cached copy of your passphrase. The cached copy is intended to make the signing and encrypting process easier on you by not requiring the passphrase to be entered for every email. PGP can be configured to cache the passphrase for only a specific amount of time or to be disabled.

After completing this lab, you will be able to:

➤ Configure PGP to disable passphrase caching

➤ Understand the PGP Single Sign-On options

Materials Required

This lab will require the following:

➤ A Windows 2000 server with Microsoft Outlook Express installed

➤ A Hotmail account with PGP installed

Estimated completion time: **15–20 minutes**

Activity

1. Launch **Outlook Express**.

2. On the Menu bar, click **Tools, PGP, Options…**.

3. Click the **General** tab.

4. Notice that **Cache passphrase for** [a certain amount of time] is selected, as shown in Figure 5-4.

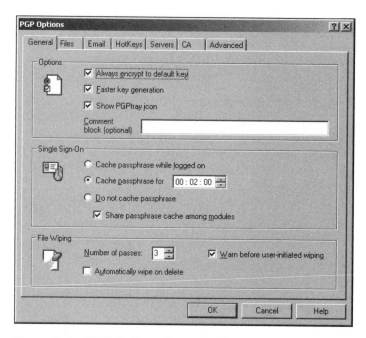

Figure 5-4   PGP Options General tab

 You can configure PGP to remember your passphrase for hours, minutes or seconds. This allows you to send multiple messages while entering the passphrase only once, but it opens a security hole.

5. Change the time to cache the passphrase to **30 minutes**.

6. Click **OK**.

7. Send two e-mails. Notice that the second e-mail did not require your passphrase to be entered.

8. On the Menu bar, click **Tools**, **PGP**, **Options…**.

9. Click the **General** tab.

10. Click the **Do not cache passphrase** radio button, as shown in Figure 5-5.

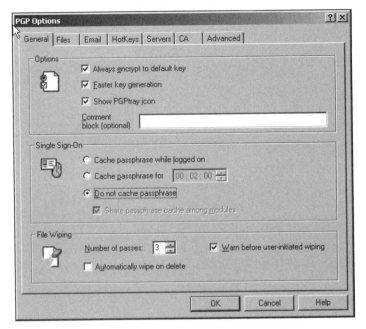

Figure 5-5   Changing the Single Sign-On options to Do not Cache Passphrase

11. Click **OK**.

12. Again, send two e-mails. Notice that this time you are required to enter your passphrase both times.

Certification Objectives

Objectives for CompTIA Security+ Exam:

➤ Communication Security: E-mail

➤ Communication Security: E-mail: PGP

Review Questions

1. Sharing your public key with other users is a security risk. True or False?

2. Sharing you private key with other users is a security risk. True or False?

3. Caching the PGP passphrase can allow another user to:

   a. send signed e-mail from your computer

   b. send signed e-mail from another computer

   c. receive e-mail from your computer

   d. receive your e-mail from another computer

4. PGP uses which of the following methods to compression routines?

   a. Zip

   b. Rar

   c. Tar

   d. Gz

5. PGP uses which of the following for symmetric encryption?

   a. DES

   b. PGP

   c. Triple DES

   d. Diffie-Hellman

LAB 5.3 EXPORTING YOUR PUBLIC KEY

Objectives

The public key system works by distributing your public key for others to encrypt data. This data can then be sent to you securely, and can be decrypted only with your private key. PGP make this process very easy by allowing you to export your public key to a text file. You can then send the public key to the person that needs to send you encrypted data. PGP also allows you to export your private key. You should be careful when doing this, as your private key should be kept secret.

After completing this lab, you will be able to:

➤ Export your public key

➤ Understand the PGP import and export processes

Materials Required

This lab will require the following:

➤ A Windows 2000 server with Microsoft Outlook Express installed

➤ A Hotmail account with PGP installed

➤ This lab should be completed with a partner who has the same materials.

Estimated completion time: **10–15 minutes**

ACTIVITY

1. Launch **Outlook Express**.

2. On the Menu bar, click **Tools**, **PGP**, **Launch PGPkeys**. The PGP Keys window will open, as shown in Figure 5-6.

Figure 5-6   PGP Keys window

3. On the Menu bar click **Keys**, **Export...**. Notice that **Include Private Key(s)** is not selected, as shown in Figure 5-7.

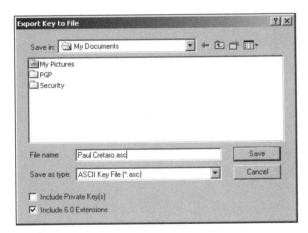

Figure 5-7   The export process for exporting a public key and/or private key

4. Click **Save** to save the file in My Documents.

5. Send an e-mail to your partner with your key attached. If you did not encrypt the attached file, you will receive the message shown in Figure 5-8.

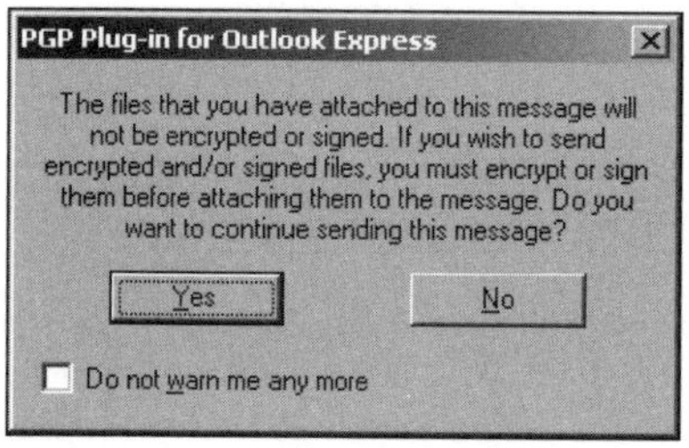

Figure 5-8 A notification that the attachment has not been encrypted

6. Click **Yes**. Enter your passphrase, and then click **OK**.

7. Once you receive the message from your partner, open the file to import the key.

8. Click the **Import** button in the select key(s) window. You will now have your partner's public key.

Certification Objectives

Objectives for CompTIA Security+ Exam:

➤ Communication Security: E-mail

Review Questions

1. Which of the following uses the same key to encrypt and decrypt?

    a. conventional cryptography

    b. traditional cryptography

    c. public key cryptography

    d. private key cryptography

2. Which of the following uses one key to encrypt and another to decrypt?

    a. conventional cryptography

    b. traditional cryptography

    c. public key cryptography

    d. private key cryptography

3. A hash function takes plain text and creates a fixed-length output regardless of the size of the message. True or False?

4. What is the result of a hash function?

    a. message

    b. message digest

    c. cipher

    d. cipher text

5. Digital Signatures provide all of the same features as encryption except privacy. True or False?

LAB 5.4 SENDING AN ANONYMOUS E-MAIL

Objectives

While there may be times that you wish to send an anonymous e-mail, you should be very careful if you decide to use this type of application. Most programs that perform this task are considered Trojan Horses by virus scanning packages. Attempting to use a Trojan Horse in a business is considered a very serious problem, and you could find yourself unemployed if you attempt to use these programs.

After completing this lab, you will be able to:

➤ Send an anonymous e-mail

➤ Understand the issues related to anonymous e-mails

Materials Required

This lab will require the following:

➤ A Windows 2000 server

➤ The MailSender e-mail program

➤ Access to an SMTP server

➤ This lab should be completed with a partner who has the same materials.

Estimated completion time: **20–30 minutes**

ACTIVITY

1. Launch MailSender. You will see a screen resembling the one shown in Figure 5-9.

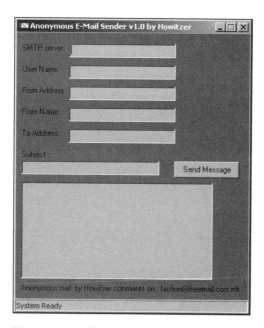

Figure 5-9   The Anonymous e-mail screen with necessary fields

2. Enter an SMTP server and username that you have access to. You can get this information from your instructor.

3. Copy the information illustrated in Figure 5-10 for the remaining fields.

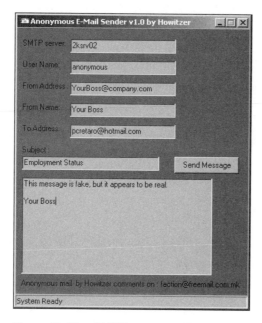

Figure 5-10   SMTP server options

4. Change the **ToAddress** to your partner's address.

5. Click **Send Message**.

6. When the message arrives, open it and notice that it appears to be legitimate.

7. Double-click **Your Boss**. Notice that the e-mail address appears to be legitimate.

8. Click **Cancel** to close Your Boss Properties.

9. Close the message.

10. With the message highlighted, click **File**, **Properties** to open the message properties.

11. Click the **Details** tab.

12. Click **Message Source...**. Examine the contents and notice that the "true" IP address, SMTP server, and user are listed.

13. Close the **Message Source** window.

14. Click **OK** to close the Message properties.

Certification Objectives

Objectives for CompTIA Security+ Exam:

➤ Communication Security: E-mail

➤ Communication Security: E-mail: Vulnerabilities

Review Questions

1. The true source of an e-mail can be found in the _____ of the message.

   a. subject

   b. attachment

   c. header

   d. body

2. Which of the following is the TCP port used by SMTP?

   a. 21

   b. 25

   c. 80

   d. 110

3. Which of the following is the TCP port used by POP3?

   a. 21

   b. 25

   c. 80

   d. 110

4. Some companies use e-mail for low-cost advertising. What is this advertising method called?

   a. mailing lists

   b. SPAM

   c. distribution groups

   d. news groups

5. File attachments are an easy way to distribute Trojan Horses, viruses, and worms. True or False?

LAB 5.5 CREATING A HIDDEN, MALICIOUS FILE ATTACHMENT

Objectives

The ability to send file attachments is one of the most useful features of e-mail. File attachments allow you to share information, such as programs, graphics, scripts, and many other types of files. Unfortunately, because of malicious attachments such as the Melissa virus and the I Love You worm, it sometimes becomes necessary to block certain types of attachments. The default settings in Microsoft Outlook block executables and scripts. Before this security feature was added to the program, it was very easy to attach a malicious file to an e-mail.

After completing this lab, you will be able to:

➤ Create a file attachment that does not appear to be what it truly is

➤ Understand the implications of sending a malicious attachment

Materials Required

This lab will require the following:

➤ A Windows 2000 server with Microsoft Outlook Express installed

➤ This lab should be completed in pairs.

Estimated completion time: **15 minutes**

ACTIVITY

1. Launch **Notepad**.

2. Enter this text: **notepad.exe**.

3. Click **File**, **Save As**.

4. Save the file as **ImportantFile.doc.bat** (but put 100 spaces after the .doc and before the .bat).

5. Save the file to My Documents.

6. Close the file.

7. Launch **Outlook Express**.

8. Send a message to your partner and attach the "ImportantFile." In the Subject field enter: **Important Document, Please Read**. You will have to enter the PGP passphrase.

9. Once the message is received, open the attachment. Note that the file appears to be a .doc file. Notepad will open.

 While the example above is not malicious, you should be aware of the possibilities. The script included in this message might well have instructed your computer to erase all files on your hard drive, for example.

Certification Objectives

Objectives for CompTIA Security+ Exam:

➤ Communication Security: E-mail

➤ Communication Security: E-mail: Vulnerabilities

Review Questions

1. PGP can protect the message but not the attachment. True or False?

2. Which of the following is a dangerous executable?

   a. exe

   b. bat

   c. vbs

   d. com

   e. all of the above

3. DES uses a _____ -bit key.

    a. 40

    b. 56

    c. 128

    d. 168

4. 3DES uses a _____ -bit key.

    a. 40

    b. 56

    c. 128

    d. 168

5. PGP and S/MIME cannot be used to decrypt both types of messages. True or False?

WEB SECURITY

Labs included in this chapter:

➤ Lab 6.1 Configuring Microsoft Internet Explorer Security

➤ Lab 6.2 Configuring Microsoft Internet Explorer Privacy

➤ Lab 6.3 Configuring Microsoft Internet Explorer Content Filtering

➤ Lab 6.4 Configuring Microsoft Internet Explorer Advanced Security Settings

➤ Lab 6.5 Manually Blocking Web Sites and Popups

CompTIA Security+ Exam Objectives	
Objective	Lab
Communication Security: Web	6.1, 6.2, 6.3, 6.4, 6.5
Communication Security: Web: HTTP/S	6.1
Communication Security: Web: Vulnerabilities: Cookies	6.2

LAB 6.1 CONFIGURING MICROSOFT INTERNET EXPLORER SECURITY

Objectives

Most large companies have advanced firewalls and proxy services that allow them to filter or block certain content from employee desktops. This is a necessary feature but it is
not always practical, especially for small- to mid-sized companies. Fortunately, Microsoft
has built-in security features available for users of Internet Explorer. In this lab, you will
configure Microsoft Internet Explorer to block cookies and file downloads with the
default settings for Restricted Sites.

After completing this lab, you will be able to:

➤ Configure Trusted Sites in Microsoft Internet Explorer 6

➤ Configure Restricted Sites to block file downloads in Microsoft Internet
Explorer 6

Materials Required

This lab will require the following:

➤ A Windows 2000 server with Microsoft Internet Explorer 6 installed

Estimated completion time: **20–25 minutes**

ACTIVITY

1. Log on as Administrator.

2. Right-click the **Internet Explorer** icon on the desktop and select
Properties.

3. Click the **Security** tab. You will see the window shown in Figure 6-1.

4. Click the **Trusted Sites** icon.

5. Click the **Default Level** button. This will set the security level for the zone
to Low.

6. Click the **Sites...** button.

7. Uncheck the **Require server verification (https:) for all sites in this
zone** option.

8. Enter the following Web sites to the zone, as shown in Figure 6-2:

www.microsoft.com

www.course.com

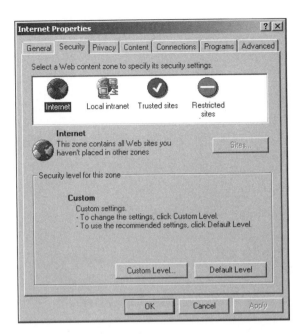

Figure 6-1   Internet Explorer Security Properties

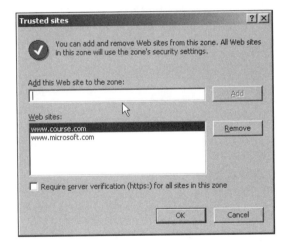

Figure 6-2   Trusted Sites

9. Click **OK**.

10. Click the **Restricted Sites** icon.

11. Click the **Sites...** button.

12. Enter the following Web sites to the zone:

   www.kazaa.com

   ftp.microsoft.com

13. Click **OK**.

14. Click **OK** to close the Internet Options Window.

15. Launch Internet Explorer.

16. Enter **www.kazaa.com** in the Address box. Notice the **Restricted sites** icon in the lower right corner of the browser. Kazaa will completely fail to load.

17. Enter **ftp.microsoft.com**.

18. Navigate to **/Reskit/win2000** and right-click **ADSizer.exe**.

19. Select **Copy to Folder....**

20. You will receive the message shown in Figure 6-3.

Figure 6-3   A message denying file downloads

 Because URLs can be redirected, this is not the best way to block file downloads. This can, however, be a helpful "quick fix."

21. Close all windows and log off.

Certification Objectives

Objectives for CompTIA Security+ Exam:

➤ Communication Security: Web: HTTP/S

Review Questions

1. Which of the following is a zone that contains all Web sites that have not been placed in other zones?

• a. Internet

   b. local intranet

   c. trusted sites

   d. restricted sites

2. Which of the following is a zone that contains Web sites that could potentially cause damage to your system?

   a. Internet

   b. local intranet

   c. trusted sites

   • d. restricted sites

3. Which of the following is a zone that contains Web sites that you believe will not cause damage to your system?

   a. Internet

   b. local intranet

   • c. trusted sites

   d. restricted sites

4. Which of the following Custom Security level settings requires a username and password for User Authentication?

   a. high

   b. medium

   c. medium–low

   d. low

   e. none of the above

5. Which of the following Custom Security level settings allows for anonymous User Authentication?

   a. high

   b. medium

   c. medium–low

   d. low

   e. none of the above

LAB 6.2 CONFIGURING MICROSOFT INTERNET EXPLORER PRIVACY

Objectives

One issue that many users have with Web browsing is the fact that anyone on the Internet has the ability to write information to their computer's hard drive. One example of this ability is the use of cookies. Cookies can be valuable to both the user and the company that deposits them. For example, if you go to an e-commerce site and fill out a form with all of your important data, a cookie can be used to remember you. This is helpful because you will not have to enter the data every time you visit the site. While this capability can be very helpful, it can also be a major security risk. With that cookie on your computer, anyone with access to your computer could go to the e-commerce site and purchase goods without your knowledge. In this lab, you will configure Internet Explorer's Privacy settings to block the use of cookies.

After completing this lab, you will be able to:

➤ Configure Microsoft Internet Explorer 6 Privacy settings

➤ Understand the different settings for cookies in Microsoft Internet Explorer 6

Materials Required

This lab will require the following:

➤ A Windows 2000 server with Microsoft Internet Explorer 6 installed

Estimated completion time: **15 minutes**

ACTIVITY

1. Log on as Administrator.

2. Right-click the **Internet Explorer** icon on the desktop and select **Properties**.

3. Click the **Privacy** tab.

4. Slide the **Settings bar** up to **High**, as shown in Figure 6-4. This will block all cookies that do not comply with the W3C P3P.

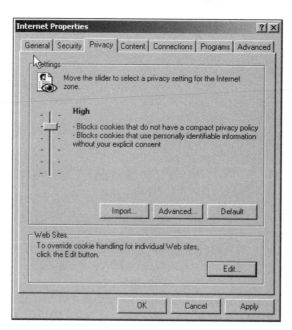

Figure 6-4   Internet Explorer Privacy Settings tab

5. Click the **Edit** button to add Web sites that you want to allow to bypass the settings.

6. Type **www.yahoo.com** in the **Address of Web Site** box.

7. Click **Allow**. Notice that only the domain is added to the Managed Web sites list, as shown in Figure 6-5.

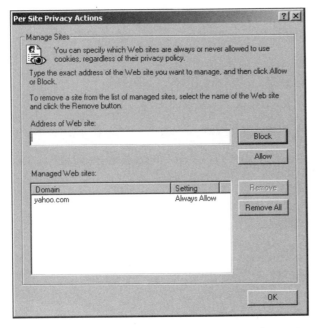

Figure 6-5   Overriding Privacy settings with Per Site Privacy Actions to allow cookies to a selected site

8. Click **OK**.

9. Click **OK**.

10. Open Internet Explorer and enter **www.msn.com** in the **Address** box.

11. Double-click the Cookie privacy warning in the toolbar, as seen in Figure 6-6.

Figure 6-6   A warning that a cookie was prevented from being copied to your computer's hard drive

12. You should receive a report similar to the one shown in Figure 6-7.

13. Click **Close**.

14. Enter **www.yahoo.com** in the Internet Explorer **Address** box. Notice that the privacy warning is absent.

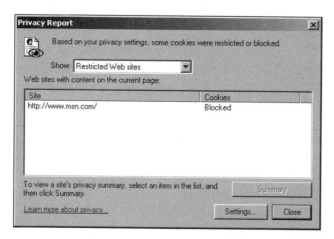

Figure 6-7   The site that was blocked from depositing a cookie on your computer

15. To reset the privacy settings, return to the **Internet Properties Privacy** tab and click the **Default** button. The settings will return to medium, the default IE setting.

Certification Objectives

Objectives for CompTIA Security+ Exam:

➤ Communication Security: Web: Vulnerabilities: Cookies

Review Questions

1. A cookie is a small text file that stores information that can be used by a server. True or False?

2. Which of the following Privacy settings will block all cookies without a Compact Privacy Policy? (Choose all that apply.)
   a. block all cookies
   b. high
   c. medium high
   d. medium
   e. low
   f. accept all cookies

3. Which of the following Privacy settings does not restrict First-party cookies?
   a. block all cookies
   b. high
   c. medium high
   d. medium

     e. low

     f. accept all cookies

4. Which of the following Privacy settings is likely to cause some Web pages to fail to load? (Choose all that apply.)

     a. block all cookies

     b. high

     c. medium high

     d. medium

     e. low

     f. accept all cookies

5. Which of the following Privacy settings is the default policy setting?

     a. block all cookies

     b. high

     c. medium high

     d. medium

     e. low

     f. accept all cookies

6

Lab 6.3 Configuring Microsoft Internet Explorer Content Filtering

Objectives

Recall that large companies can filter content by using a proxy server. Internet Explorer can also filter content based on RSACi settings. The Recreational Software Advisory Council (RSAC), which has become the Internet Content Rating Association (ICRA), is an independent organization that works to protect children from potentially harmful material on the Internet. RSACi is their content rating system for Internet sites. The categories that can be filtered are Language, Nudity, Sex, and Violence. Each of these categories can be individually configured to meet the needs of the users.

After completing this lab, you will be able to:

➤ Configure content filtering in Microsoft Internet Explorer 6

➤ Password protect the content filtering settings

Materials Required

This lab will require the following:

➤ A Windows 2000 server with Microsoft Internet Explorer 6 installed

Estimated completion time: **15–20 minutes**

ACTIVITY

1. Log on as Administrator.

2. Right-click the **Internet Explorer** icon on the desktop and select **Properties**.

3. Click the **Content** tab. You will see a screen similar to the one shown in Figure 6-8.

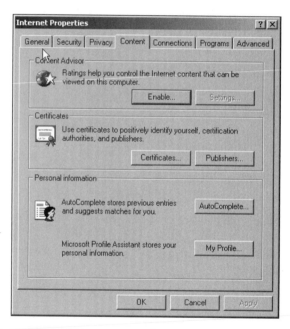

Figure 6-8   Internet Explorer Content Settings tab

4. In the **Content Advisor** section, click **Enable**.

5. The Content Advisor window will pop up, as shown in Figure 6-9.

6. Leave all of the settings at **Level 0**; this is the most restrictive setting. You may want to slide the bars for each of the categories to see what each level will allow.

7. Click the **General** tab, as shown in Figure 6-10.

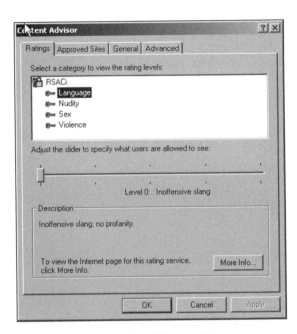

Figure 6-9   Content Advisor settings

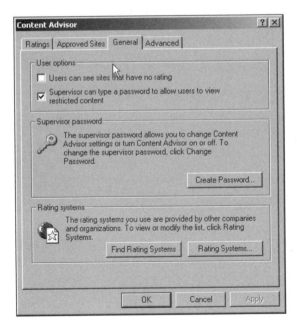

Figure 6-10   Content Advisor Supervisor password option

8. Click the **Create Password...** button, as shown in Figure 6-11.

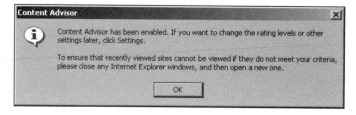

Figure 6-11   Creating a supervisor password

9. Use **password** as the password.

10. Enter **Course** for the Hint.

11. Click **OK**.

12. You will receive a message telling you that the supervisor password was success-fully created.

13. Click **OK**.

14. Click **OK** to close the Content Advisor.

15. You will receive the message shown in Figure 6-12.

Figure 6-12   Content Advisor enabled warning message

16. Click **OK**.

17. Click **OK** to close the Internet Properties dialog box.

18. Launch Internet Explorer.

19. Enter **www.nick.com** (a children's site from Nickelodeon). You will receive the message shown in Figure 6-13.

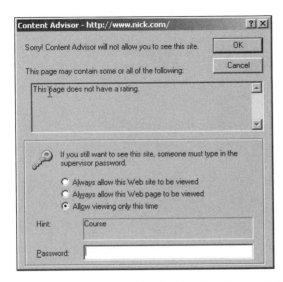

Figure 6-13   A site blocked by the Content Advisor

20. Enter **password** in the Password box and you will be granted access to the site. Note: These settings are very restrictive, and you may be prompted multiple times per site.

21. Return to the **Content** tab of the Internet properties and click **Disable**.

22. You will be prompted to enter the password. Enter **password**. Click **OK**.

23. You will receive the message shown in Figure 6-14.

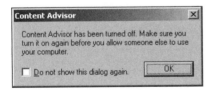

Figure 6-14   A message when the Content Advisor has been turned off

24. Click **OK**.

25. Click **OK** to close the Internet Properties.

26. Close Internet Explorer and log off.

Certification Objectives

Objectives for CompTIA Security+ Exam:

➤ Communication Security: Web

Review Questions

1. Which of the follow is the most restrictive rating level?

   a. Level 0

   b. Level 1

   c. Level 2

   d. Level 3

   e. Level 4

2. A way to bypass the Ratings settings is to:

   a. allow the Web site in the Advanced settings

   b. allow the Web site in the Approved sites list

   c. allow the Web site in the Allowed sites list

   d. You cannot override the Ratings settings.

3. The Supervisor can access restricted sites by entering the Supervisor password. True or False?

4. What is the default response by the Content Advisor if the Web site does not have a rating?

   a. The user will be able to view the page.

   b. The user will be unable to view the page.

   c. The user will be able to view the page by manually entering a rating.

   d. none of the above

5. You just configured the Content Advisor settings; all but one of the computers on the network appears to bypass the rules. What could be the problem?

   a. The rules were configured incorrectly.

   b. You forgot to apply the rules.

   c. The site that was allowed was not rated.

   d. The Temporary Internet Files have not been deleted.

LAB 6.4 CONFIGURING MICROSOFT INTERNET EXPLORER ADVANCED SECURITY SETTINGS

Objectives

In addition to cookies, Internet Explorer can store information about your Web browsing habits by caching. This can be a major problem in areas that require high level security. Most users are aware of Temporary Internet Files and how to remove them. Temporary Internet Files are used as a local cache to increase the speed of Web browsing, but the files can also be used to track your path on the Web. Usernames and passwords can also be stored to save you time, but this may also allow for unauthorized access to resources. Fortunately, these issues can be resolved by using Internet Explorer's Advanced Security Settings.

After completing this lab, you will be able to:

➤ Configure the Advanced Settings in Microsoft Internet Explorer 6

➤ Protect your information related to Web browsing

Materials Required

This lab will require the following:

➤ A Windows 2000 server with Microsoft Internet Explorer 6 installed

6

Estimated completion time: **10 minutes**

ACTIVITY

1. Log on as Administrator.

2. Right-click the **Internet Explorer** icon on the desktop and select **Properties**.

3. Click the **Advanced** tab.

4. Scroll down to the **Security Settings**, as shown in Figure 6-15.

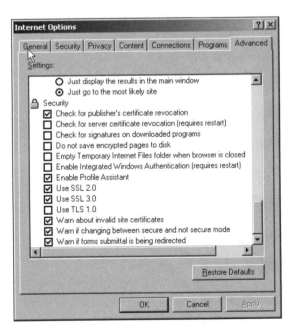

Figure 6-15   Advanced Internet Security Options

5. Check the **Empty Temporary Internet Files folder when browser is closed** option.

6. Click the **Content** tab.

7. Click the **AutoComplete...** button.

8. Uncheck the box in **Use AutoComplete for Usernames and passwords on forms**, as shown in Figure 6-16.

Figure 6-16   Auto Complete Options

9. Click **OK** to close the AutoComplete Settings window.

10. Click **OK** to close the Internet Options window.

11. Close all remaining windows and log off.

Certification Objectives

Objectives for CompTIA Security+ Exam:

➤ Communication Security: Web

Review Questions

1. If you wish to prevent secure files from being stored in Temporary Internet Files you can check which of the following Security options?

   a. Do not save encrypted file to disk.

   b. Empty Temporary Internet Files folder when browser is closed.

   c. Use Fortezza.

   d. Do not save Certificates to disk.

2. When you enable the option *Empty Temporary Internet Files folder when your browser is closed*, it also deletes all cookies. True or False?

3. All secure Web sites support which of the following protocols?

   a. SSL 2.0

   b. SSL 3.0

   c. TLS 1.0

   d. PCT 1.0

4. Which of the following protocols was developed by Microsoft?

   a. SSL 2.0

   b. SSL 3.0

   c. TLS 1.0

   d. PCT 1.0

5. Which of the following protocols requires a Crypto Card?

   a. EFS

   b. Fortezza

   c. Crypto

   d. TLS 1.0

6

LAB 6.5 MANUALLY BLOCKING WEB SITES AND POPUPS

Objectives

One of the most useful, yet annoying features of Web browsing is the "popup." Popups can be a very effective form of advertising, but at the same time, they can be very annoying to the user accessing the Web site. There are a few commercial and freeware products that can block popups. None of these methods works 100% of the time. Another quick and easy method that can be used is to redirect the Web site to the local loopback. This method can be used to both disable popups and to block access to Web sites. This method utilizes the local hosts file.

After completing this lab, you will be able to:

➤ Edit the hosts file to redirect Web sites and prevent access to that site

➤ Edit the hosts file to stop popup ads

Materials Required

This lab will require the following:

➤ A Windows 2000 server with Microsoft Internet Explorer 6 installed

Estimated completion time: **20 minutes**

ACTIVITY

1. Log on as Administrator.

2. Click **Start**, **Search**, **For Files or Folders...**.

3. Type **hosts**.

4. Click **Search now**.

5. The results should be similar to the screen shown in Figure 6-17.

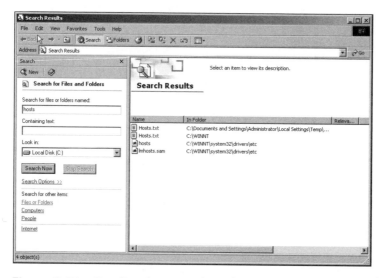

Figure 6-17　Results when searching for the hosts file on a Windows 2000 Server

6. Right-click the **hosts** file that is located in **%systemroot%\system32\drivers\etc**.

7. Select **Open with...**.

8. Choose **Notepad** and click **OK**.

9. Add the following line to the end of the file, as shown in Figure 6-18:

   127.0.0.2　　　　www.yahoo.com

10. Save and close the **hosts** file.

11. Open **Internet Explorer** and try to go to **www.yahoo.com**.

12. Your computer now thinks www.yahoo.com is located on itself and will fail to load. If Yahoo loads it may be in your cache. Click **Refresh** to get the error.

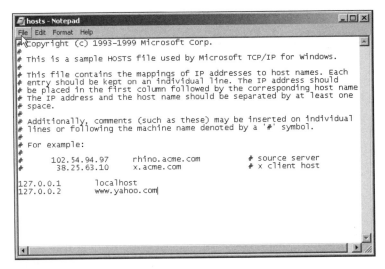

Figure 6-18 A sample hosts file with an additional site added

 Don't forget to undo these steps before moving on!

To apply this method to popups:

1. When a popup appears on the screen, right-click it and select **Properties**.

2. Make a note of the server and domain name, for example, **ads.x10.com**.

3. Add the address to the hosts file and it will prevent the popups.

Certification Objectives

Objectives for CompTIA Security+ Exam:

➤ Communication Security: Web

REVIEW QUESTIONS

1. The hosts file resolves:

   a. IP address–to–host name

   b. IP address–to–NetBIOS name

   c. IP address–to–MAC address

   d. host name–to–IP address

2. You recently made some changes to the hosts file on your computer, but they do not seem to be working. What could be the problem?

a. The changes were overruled by DNS.

b. The hosts file is not used if you are configured to use DNS.

c. You made the changes in a text editor that appended .txt to the file.

d. You made the changes in a spreadsheet application that appended .csv to the file.

3. You recently changed the IP address of a mail server. Now some remote users cannot access their e-mail. What is the likely cause?

a. They did not change their e-mail setting to reflect the IP address change.

b. DNS is not configured properly.

c. They have an entry in the hosts file with the old IP address.

d. They deleted their hosts file.

4. Which of the following is an advantage to blocking Web sites with the hosts file?

a. The site cannot put a cookie on your computer.

b. It will prevent your computer from ever going to the ad servers.

c. The ad servers cannot profile you.

d. all of the above

5. A host file can be used to increase Web browsing speed. True or False?

CHAPTER SEVEN

DIRECTORY AND FILE TRANSFER SERVICES

Labs included in this chapter:

➤ Lab 7.1 Installing an FTP Server on Windows 2000

➤ Lab 7.2 Creating a New FTP Site

➤ Lab 7.3 Controlling Access to the FTP Site

➤ Lab 7.4 Creating FTP Messages

➤ Lab 7.5 Configuring FTP TCP/IP Restrictions

CompTIA Security+ Exam Objectives	
Objective	Lab
Communication Security: File Transfer: S/FTP	7.1, 7.2, 7.3, 7.4, 7.5
Communication Security: File Transfer: Blind FTP/Anonymous	7.3
Communication Security: File Transfer: Vulnerabilities: Packet Sniffing	7.3, 7.5

Lab 7.1 Installing an FTP Server on Windows 2000

Objectives

File Transfer Protocol (FTP) is a very useful TCP/IP protocol used for transferring files across the Internet. Today, most e-mail packages have the ability to send files, but are usually limited by size at the mail server. Many professionals would recommend using FTP instead of e-mail when the attachments exceed 1MB. At the same time, most of the data that travels across the Internet is much larger than 1MB. Windows 2000 has the ability to act as an FTP client and server.

After completing this lab, you will be able to:

➤ Install FTP on a Windows 2000 server

➤ Understand the security risk in having the FTP server service installed

Materials Required

This lab will require the following:

➤ Two Windows 2000 servers

➤ Administrator access to both servers

➤ The Windows 2000 Server CD

Estimated completion time: **15 minutes**

Activity

This lab must be completed in pairs. The servers used in this activity will be referred to as Server-X and Server-Y. Please substitute the names of your servers for these names.

1. On Server-Y, click **Start, Run,** and type **cmd**. Press **Enter**.

2. Type **ftp** at the command line and press **Enter**.

3. At the ftp prompt type **open server-x** and then press **Enter**. Your connection will be refused.

4. Type quit and close the command window.

5. On Server-X, click **Start, Settings, Control Panel**.

6. Double-click **Add/Remove Programs**.

7. Click **Add/Remove Windows Components**.

8. Click and highlight **Internet Information Services (IIS)**, as shown in Figure 7–1.

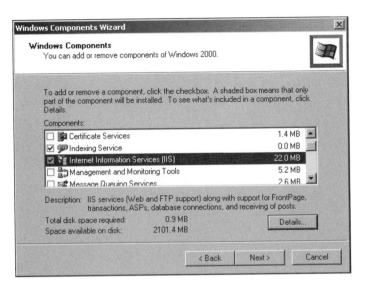

Figure 7-1 Windows Networking Components

9. Click the **Details** button.

10. Click the **File Transfer Protocol (FTP) Server** box.

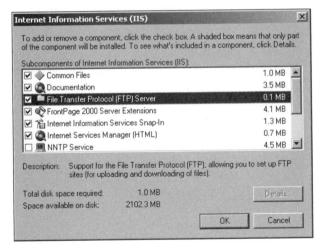

Figure 7-2 Internet Information Services Components

11. Click **OK**.

12. Click **Next** to start the installation. If promted, insert the Windows 2000 Server CD into the CD-ROM drive, and click **OK**.

13. Once the installation is complete, click **Finish**.

14. Close the **Add/Remove Programs** window.

15. Close the **Control Panel** window. The FTP server is now installed.

Certification Objectives

Objectives for CompTIA Security+ Exam:

➤ Communication Security: File Transfer: S/FTP

Review Questions

1. The Windows 2000 FTP Server Service is available only for the Server line. True or False?

2. Which of the following commands is used to connect to an ftp server?

   a. connect

   b. attach

   c. open

   d. login

3. Which of the following commands are used to copy files to a server? (Choose all that apply.)

   a. copy

   b. put

   c. xcopy

   d. mput

4. Which of the following commands are used to download files from a server? (Choose all that apply.)

   a. copy

   b. xcopy

   c. get

   d. mget

5. Which of the following commands will end a session and close ftp?

   a. exit

   b. logoff

   c. quit

   d. logout

LAB 7.2 CREATING A NEW FTP SITE

Objectives

After installing FTP, it is important to create an FTP site so that the management of the data can be controlled. An open FTP site requires heavy monitoring to prevent the transfer of dangerous files, such as viruses and Trojan Horses. When you create a site, you need to determine the access type, and if it will be a read-only site. Most sites intended for sharing files use anonymous read-only access. This will allow anyone to download the data but prevent them from uploading anything.

After completing this lab, you will be able to:

➤ Create a new FTP site on a Windows 2000 server

➤ Access the new FTP site from a client

Materials Required

This lab will require the following:

➤ Two Windows 2000 servers, one with the FTP service installed

➤ Administrator access to both servers

➤ A folder called ftp located in the root directory

Estimated completion time: 15–20 minutes

ACTIVITY

This lab requires the use of two servers, one of which has the FTP service installed. The servers are designated Server-X and Server-Y. Server-X is the server with FTP installed.

1. On Server-X (the FTP server), right-click **My Computer** and select **Manage**.

2. Expand **Services and Applications**.

3. Expand **Internet Information Services**, as shown in Figure 7-3.

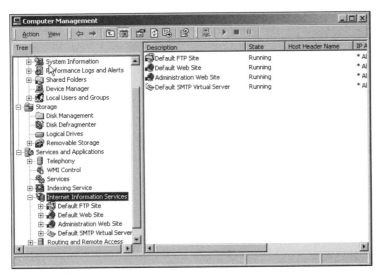

Figure 7-3   Internet Information Services Snap-in accessed from Computer Management

4. Right-click **Internet Information Services**, select **New**, then click **FTP Site**. The FTP Site Creation Wizard will begin.

5. Click **Next**.

6. Enter a **Description** (you can use **My FTP Site**), and then click **Next**.

7. Keep the default settings for the **IP Address and TCP Port Settings** step and click **Next**.

8. In the **FTP Site Home Directory** box, type **e:\ftp** drive, as shown in Figure 7-4. If your root directory is different than e:\, substitute the root directory on your system.

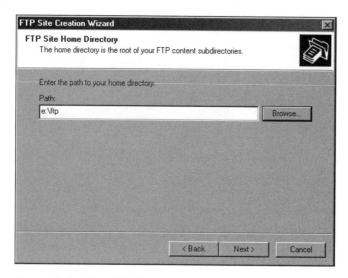

Figure 7-4   The FTP Site Home Directory box

9. Click **Next**.

10. Check the **Write** box on the **FTP Site Access Permissions** step, then click **Next**.

11. Click **Finish** to close the Wizard. Notice your ftp site is stopped, as shown in Figure 7-5.

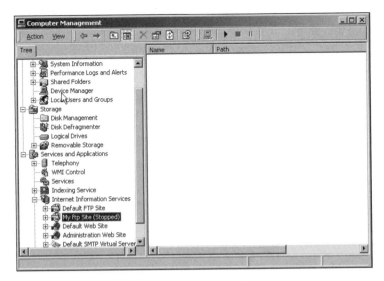

Figure 7-5   The New ftp site shown to be stopped

12. To start your ftp server you will have to first stop the Default FTP Site.

13. Right-click **Default FTP Site**, then select **Stop**.

14. Right-click **My FTP Site**, then select **Start**.

15. On Server-Y, click **Start**, **Run**, and type **cmd**.

16. Type **ftp** at the command line and press **Enter**.

17. At the ftp prompt type **open server-x**, then press **Enter**.

18. Enter **anonymous** for the username, then press **Enter**.

19. Enter **password** for the password, then press **Enter**. You will be connected.

20. Type **quit** and press **Enter** to end the ftp session.

Certification Objectives

Objectives for CompTIA Security+ Exam:

➤ Communication Security: File Transfer: S/FTP

Review Questions

1. What are the default access permissions for a new ftp site in Windows 2000?

   a. everyone full control

   b. everyone no access

   c. anonymous connections allowed

   d. anonymous connections denied

2. Which of the following ports is used by ftp for session control and data transfer? (Choose all that apply.)

   a. 20

   b. 21

   c. 22

   d. 23

3. What is the correct format of the anonymous user account?

   a. IUSR_Server_name

   b. FUSR_Server_name

   c. Anonymous

   d. Guest

4. By default Windows 2000 ftp Server will allow only anonymous connections. True or False?

5. The location of the default FTP Site is:

   a. \inetpub\ftp

   b. \ftproot

   c. \inetpub\ftproot

   d. \winnt\ftproot

Lab 7.3 Controlling Access to the FTP Site

Objectives

The default setting for an FTP site is to allow anonymous access. However, there are times when it is necessary to control access. The Windows 2000 FTP Server service has capabilities to remove anonymous access and require user authentication. The major risk when switching to authentication is that the usernames and passwords are sent in clear text, which can be sniffed with a protocol analyzer.

After completing this lab, you will be able to:

> ➤ Control access to your FTP site

> ➤ Understand the risks involved with removing anonymous access to the site

Materials Required

This lab will require the following:

> ➤ Two Windows 2000 servers, one with the FTP service installed

> ➤ Administrator access to both servers

> ➤ An active FTP site

Estimated completion time: **15–20 minutes**

ACTIVITY

This lab requires the use of two servers, one of which has the FTP service installed. The servers are designated Server-X and Server-Y. Server-X is the server with FTP installed.

1. On Server-X (the FTP server), right-click **My Computer** and select **Manage**.

2. Expand **Services and Applications**.

3. Expand **Internet Information Services**.

4. Right-click **My FTP Site** and select **Properties**.

5. Click the **Security Accounts** tab.

6. Uncheck the **Allow Anonymous Connections** box. You will receive the message shown in Figure 7-6.

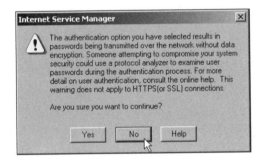

Figure 7-6   Warning message about ftp sending usernames and passwords in plain text

7. Click **Yes**.

Anonymous access will no longer be allowed, but there is a risk of having the password sniffed on the network.

8. Click **Apply**.

9. On Server-Y, click **Start**, **Run**, and type **cmd**. Press **Enter**.

10. Type **ftp** at the command line and press **Enter**.

11. At the ftp prompt type **open server-x**.

12. Enter **anonymous** for the username, and then press **Enter**.

13. Enter **password** for the password and press **Enter**. The login will fail because a valid account with a password is required.

14. At the ftp prompt type **user** then press **Enter**.

15. Type **user1** for the Username then press **Enter**.

16. Type the password for the User 1 account, and then press **Enter**.

17. You will be connected.

18. Type **quit** to end the ftp session.

Certification Objectives

Objectives for CompTIA Security+ Exam:

➤ Communication Security: File Transfer: S/FTP

➤ Communication Security: File Transfer: Blind FTP/Anonymous

➤ Communication Security: File Transfer: Vulnerabilities: Packet Sniffing

Review Questions

1. Using FTP without anonymous connections can be a security risk because it sends the username and password in plain text. True or False?

2. When the Allow IIS to control password box is checked, the password settings will be synchronized with Windows. True or False?

3. The administrators of an FTP site in Windows 2000 are known as:

   a. administrators

   b. supervisors

   c. FTP site operators

   d. FTP administrators

4. What are the default file permissions for a Windows 2000 FTP server? (Choose all that apply.)

   a. read

   b. write

   c. full control

   d. log visits

5. Which of the following are available Directory Style Listings? (Choose all that apply.)

   a. Windows NT

   b. MS-DOS

   c. UNIX

   d. Linux

LAB 7.4 CREATING FTP MESSAGES

Objectives

When you connect to an FTP site, it usually leaves you at a command line with no guidance. One of the features of the Windows 2000 FTP Server service is the ability to provide an opening and closing message. The opening message can contain any text and can be used for a simple hello, site instructions, or a disclaimer. The closing message can be used to say goodbye or provide further instructions. While these messages are not required, they can be helpful to the user trying to access the site.

After completing this lab, you will be able to:

➤ Create a message for an FTP site

Materials Required

This lab will require the following:

➤ Two Windows 2000 Servers, one with the FTP service installed

➤ Administrator access to both servers

➤ An active FTP site

Estimated completion time: **10–15 minutes**

ACTIVITY

This lab requires the use of two servers, one of which has the FTP service installed. The servers are designated Server-X and Server-Y. Server-X is the server with FTP installed.

1. On Server-X (the FTP server), right-click **My Computer** and select **Manage**.

2. Expand **Services and Applications**.

3. Expand **Internet Information Services**.

4. Right-click **My FTP Site** and select **Properties**.

5. Click the **Messages** tab.

6. Enter the following text in the **Welcome** pane:

   Hello!

   Welcome to My ftp Site.

   Please feel free to download anything you can use.

7. Enter the following text in the **Exit** pane:

   Goodbye!!! Come Back Soon.

8. Your screen should resemble the one shown in Figure 7-7.

9. Click **Apply** and then click **OK**.

10. On Server-Y, click **Start**, **Run**, and type **cmd**. Press **Enter**.

11. Type **ftp** at the command line and press **Enter**.

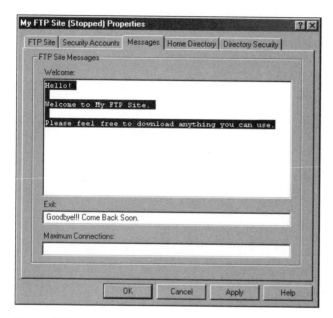

Figure 7-7 Messages tab of the new ftp Site Properties

12. At the ftp prompt type **open server-x**.

13. Enter **user1** for the username, and then press **Enter**.

14. Enter the password for the User 1 account, and press **Enter**. The welcome message is displayed.

15. Type **quit** to end the session. Notice the closing message.

Certification Objectives

Objectives for CompTIA Security+ Exam:

➤ Communication Security: File Transfer: S/FTP

Review Questions

1. When will the exit message appear? (Choose all that apply.)

   a. when a user quits

   b. when a user logs off

   c. when a user disconnects

   d. when a user types "bye" to exit a session

2. When will the welcome message appear?

   a. when a user logs on

   b. when a user connects to a server

   c. when a user disconnects from a server

   d. when a user first tries to access a directory

3. What is the default welcome message?

   a. hello

   b. welcome

   c. blank

   d. none of the above

4. What does the Maximum Connections field provide?

   a. displays a message when a user has exceeded the maximum number of connections allowed

   b. displays a message when the service has reached the maximum number of connections allowed

   c. actually determines how many sessions a user can have open at one time

   d. displays a message when the user logs off of the server

5. By default, all messages are left blank. True or False?

LAB 7.5 CONFIGURING FTP TCP/IP RESTRICTIONS

Objectives

As mentioned before, removing anonymous access to an FTP site makes it vulnerable to password sniffing. One way to counter this vulnerability is to restrict access to the site by IP address. A user trying to access the site would have to provide a valid username and password, and would have to access the site from the appropriate computer. This method can be very effective in preventing someone on the outside from using a sniffer to obtain a username and password and unauthorized access to an FTP site.

After completing this lab, you will be able to:

➤ Restrict access to your FTP site by IP address

➤ Use the TCP/IP restrictions to secure your FTP site

Materials Required

This lab will require the following:

➤ Two Windows 2000 servers, one with the FTP service installed

➤ Administrator access to both servers

➤ An active FTP site

Estimated completion time: **10–15 minutes**

ACTIVITY

This lab requires the use of two servers, one of which has the FTP service installed. The servers are designated Server-X and Server-Y. Server-X is the server with FTP installed.

1. On Server-X (the FTP server), right-click **My Computer** and select **Manage**.

2. Expand **Services and Applications**.

3. Expand **Internet Information Services**.

4. Right-click **My FTP Site** and select **Properties**.

5. Click the **Directory Security** tab.

6. Click the **Denied Access** radio button.

7. Click **Add**.

8. Enter the IP address of Server-Y, and then click **OK**.

9. Your Directory Security tab should resemble the one in Figure 7-8.

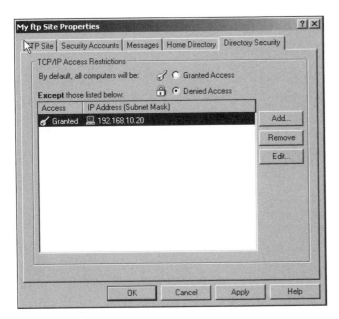

Figure 7-8   Directory Security for the new ftp site

10. Click the **Granted Access** radio button.

11. Click **Add**.

12. Enter the IP address of the Instructor's server, and then click **OK**.

13. Click **Apply**, and then click **OK**.

14. On Server-Y, click **Start**, **Run**, and type **cmd**. Press **Enter**.

15. Type **ftp** at the command line and press **Enter**.

16. At the **ftp** prompt type **open server-x**.

17. Type the password for the User 1 account, and then press **Enter**.

18. Enter **Password1** for the password. You will be denied access because your IP address has been denied access.

19. Type **quit** to end the session. Notice that the Closing message still appears.

20. Close all windows and log off.

21. Ask the instructor to attempt to access your FTP server. The connection will be successful.

Certification Objectives

Objectives for CompTIA Security+ Exam:

➤ Communication Security: File Transfer: S/FTP

➤ Communication Security: File Transfer: Vulnerabilities: Packet Sniffing

Review Questions

1. What are the options available for TCP/IP Access Restrictions? (Choose all that apply.)

   a. granted access

   b. enable access

   c. denied access

   d. full access

2. If an IP address has been denied access, a user can still attach to the FTP server. True or False?

3. If an IP address has been denied access to an FTP server:

   a. Users can logon using the administrator password.

   b. Users can logon using their password.

   c. Users can logon using an Anonymous account.

   d. Users will not be able to access the server.

4. By default, all IP addresses are granted access. True or False?

5. Computers trying to access the FTP server through a proxy server will not be able to be individually denied access because they access the FTP server with the IP address of the proxy server. True or False?

CHAPTER EIGHT

WIRELESS AND INSTANT MESSAGING

Labs included in this chapter:

➤ Lab 8.1 Installing the Cisco Aironet 340 Wireless Access Point

➤ Lab 8.2 Disabling Telnet Access to the Aironet WAP

➤ Lab 8.3 Enabling the Aironet User Manager

➤ Lab 8.4 Adding Administrative Users to the Aironet

➤ Lab 8.5 Restoring Aironet Factory Default Settings

CompTIA Security+ Exam Objectives	
Objective	Lab
Communication Security: Wireless	8.1, 8.2, 8.3, 8.4, 8.5
Communication Security: Wireless: WEP/WAP	8.1, 8.2, 8.3, 8.4, 8.5

Lab 8.1 Installing the Cisco Aironet 340 Wireless Access Point

Objectives

Access to a network is essential for most employees in companies, particularly for IT professionals. For those IT professionals that use a laptop computer in multiple locations, a network connection is not always available. In these cases, wireless access is a convenient tool. In this lab you will install the Cisco Aironet 340 Wireless Access Point (WAP), which allows laptops and other mobile computer systems wireless access to a network.

After completing this lab, you will be able to:

➤ Install a Cisco Aironet 340 Wireless Access Point

➤ Configure the SSID and Radio Channel for the Cisco Aironet 340 WAP

Materials Required

This lab will require the following:

➤ A Windows 2000 server

➤ A DHCP server

➤ A Cisco Aironet 340 WAP

Estimated completion time: **20–25 minutes**

 ## Activity

1. Connect the Cisco 340 Aironet to a power source and then connect it to your Ethernet-based network.

2. Identify the MAC address assigned to the Aironet device. Note: the MAC address can be found on the bottom of the Aironet.

3. Ask the instructor what IP address is assigned to the MAC address of your Aironet.

4. If you are running DHCP on your server, check the Unique ID field in the DHCP Manager for the MAC Address, as shown in Figure 8-1. Note: You may have to scroll to the right to see the field.

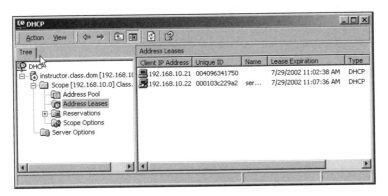

Figure 8-1   Windows 2000 DHCP Manager

   5. Launch **Internet Explorer**.

   6. Enter the IP address of the Aironet in the **Address** box and then press **Enter**. You should see the screen shown in Figure 8-2.

8

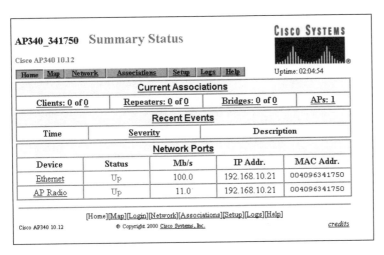

Figure 8-2   Cisco Aironet 340 opening screen

   7. Click the **AP Radio** link. You will see a screen similar to the one shown Figure 8-3.

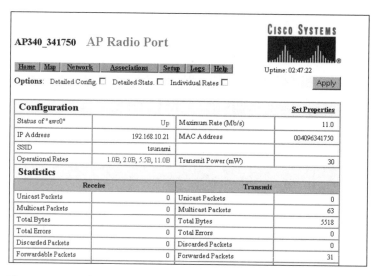

Figure 8-3   The AP Radio Link

8. Click the **Set Properties** link. You will see a screen similar to the one shown in Figure 8-4.

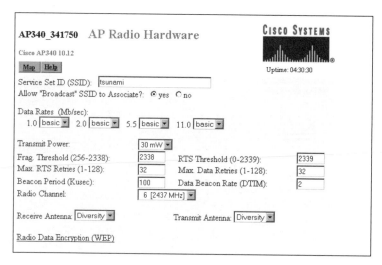

Figure 8-4   AP Radio Port properties screen

9. Note that the default SSID is **tsunami**. To assign a unique identity to this WLAN, change this value.

10. Also make a note of the Radio Channel. If you have a 2.4 GHz cordless phone, the channels can interfere with each other. You can adjust this value to 1 through 11.

11. Click **OK**. You will receive the message shown in Figure 8-5.

Figure 8-5 Warning message

12. Click **OK**.

13. Close your Web browser.

Certification Objectives

Objectives for CompTIA Security+ Exam:

➤ Communication Security: Wireless

➤ Communication Security: Wireless: WEP/WAP

Review Questions

1. Which of the following can be used to access the Cisco Aironet WAP?

   a. Telnet

   b. serial

   c. Ethernet

   d. HTTP

   e. all of the above

2. Which of the following requires direct access to the Cisco Aironet WAP?

   a. Telnet

   b. serial

   c. Ethernet

   d. HTTP

3. The default configuration of the Cisco Aironet allows everyone access to the system configuration. True or False?

4. Which of the following is a setting used for terminal connections?

   a. 8 data bits

   b. 9600 bits per second

   c. 1 stop bit

   d. no parity

   e. XON/XOFF flow control

5. The Cisco Aironet operates at 2.4 GHz and can conflict with certain cordless phones. True or False?

Lab 8.2 Disabling Telnet Access to the Aironet WAP

Objectives

Telnet is a very useful TCP/IP utility, but it has security holes. One major security flaw is that it sends passwords across the wire in plain text. To be safe, you can disable Telnet directly from the Cisco Aironet. Removing Telnet access to the Aironet will make the administration a little more difficult by removing that method of administrative access, but it will help to further secure the device. HTTP access will be an available administrative access method once this is complete.

After completing this lab, you will be able to:

➤ Access the Cisco Aironet Setup screen

➤ Disable Telnet access to the WAP

Materials Required

This lab will require the following:

➤ A Windows 2000 server

➤ DHCP server

➤ A Cisco Aironet 340 WAP

Estimated completion time: **10–15 minutes**

Activity

1. On your server, click **Start, Run** and type **cmd** at the command line. Press **Enter**.

2. Enter **telnet 192.168.10.21** (replace this address with the address of your Aironet).

3. Press **Enter**. Note that you were able to connect.

4. Close the command window.

5. Launch **Internet Explorer**.

6. Enter the IP address of the Aironet in the **Address** box and then press **Enter**.

7. Click the **Setup** link to enter the Setup screen. This screen is shown in Figure 8-6.

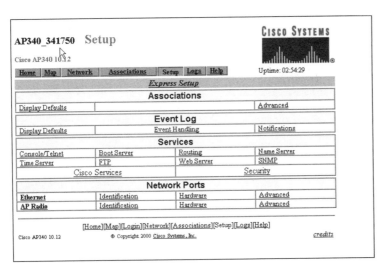

Figure 8-6   Aironet 340 Setup screen

8. Under Services click the **Console/Telnet** link.

9. Click the **Disabled** radio button, as shown in Figure 8-7.

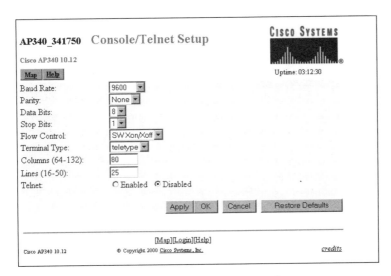

Figure 8-7   Aironet 340 Console/Telnet configuration screen

10. Click **OK**. You will receive the message shown in Figure 8-8.

Figure 8-8   Warning message

11. Click **OK**. The setting will be saved and you will return to the Setup screen.

12. Click **Start**, **Run** and type **cmd** at the command line. Press **Enter**.

13. Type **telnet 192.168.10.21** (replace this address with the address of your Aironet), and press **Enter**. You will receive the message "Connection to host lost". Telnet access is now disabled.

14. Close the command window, and then close **Internet Explorer**.

Certification Objectives

Objectives for CompTIA Security+ Exam:

➤ Communication Security: Wireless

➤ Communication Security: Wireless: WEP/WAP

Review Questions

1. Which of the following can be used to configure the Cisco Aironet in a text-based environment?

   a. Telnet

   b. FTP

   c. TFTP

   d. HTTP

2. Which of the following can be used to configure the Cisco Aironet in a GUI environment?

   a. Telnet

   b. FTP

   c. TFTP

   d. HTTP

3. Telnet is disabled by default on the Cisco Aironet. True or False?

4. Telnet can be a security risk because it transmits the username and password in clear text. True or False?

5. Which of the following TCP ports does Telnet use?

    a. 20

    b. 21

    c. 23

    d. 25

LAB 8.3 ENABLING THE AIRONET USER MANAGER

Objectives

The default setting of the Cisco Aironet 340 is to allow all users access to the configuration utilities, which is convenient for initial setup and configuration. Once the device is ready for production, however, you should control access. If you fail to change this configuration, you run the risk of handing a cracker the key to your wireless network. To limit access to the configuration utilities you must enable the User Manager, change the Administrator password, and add additional accounts. Be sure to remember that the account names are case-sensitive and that if you forget the passwords, you will have to use the serial port access to reset the device.

After completing this lab, you will be able to:

➤ Enable the Cisco Aironet 340 WAP User Manager

➤ Configure password access to the Cisco Aironet 340 WAP

Materials Required

This lab will require the following:

➤ A Windows 2000 server

➤ DHCP server

➤ A Cisco Aironet 340 WAP

Estimated completion time: **10–15 minutes**

ACTIVITY

1. Launch **Internet Explorer**.

2. Enter the IP address of the Aironet in the Address box and then press **Enter**.

3. Click the **Setup** link.

4. Under Services, click the **Security** link. You will see the screen shown in Figure 8-9.

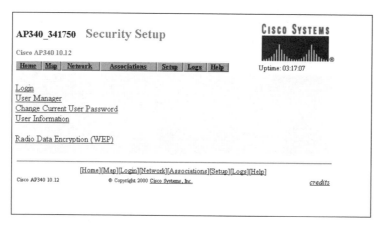

Figure 8-9   Aironet 340 Security Setup screen

5. Click the User Information link.

6. Click the **Administrator** link.

7. Set the user name to **Administrator** and the password to **password**.

8. Select all of the boxes under the **capability settings**, as shown in Figure 8-10.

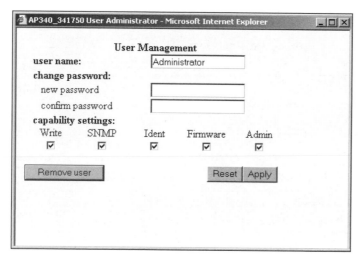

Figure 8-10   Administrator properties in the User Manager

9. Click **Apply**.

10. Click the **Back** button in Internet Explorer.

11. Click the **User Manager** link. You will see the screen shown in Figure 8-11.

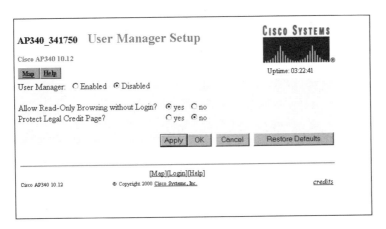

Figure 8-11   Aironet 340 User Manager Setup screen

8

12. Click the **Enabled** radio button to enable the User Manager.

13. Click the **no** radio button for the **Allow Read-Only Browsing without Login** option.

14. Click **OK**; you will be prompted to OK the changes.

15. Click **OK**.

16. Close **Internet Explorer**.

17. Launch **Internet Explorer**.

18. Enter the IP address of the Aironet in the Address box and then press **Enter**. You will now have to log in to access the Aironet settings.

19. Log on as Administrator. (Note: the username is case-sensitive on this device.)

20. Close **Internet Explorer**.

Certification Objectives

Objectives for CompTIA Security+ Exam:

➤ Communication Security: Wireless

➤ Communication Security: Wireless: WEP/WAP

Review Questions

1. When limiting access to configuration utilities, which of the following should be changed, in addition to adding users? (Choose all that apply.)

   a. the MAC address

   b. the default account and password

   c. the IP address

   d. the SSID

2. One way to secure a wireless network is to use a:
   a. firewall
   b. scrambler
   c. VPN
   d. DMZ

3. One way to secure the wireless administration of a Cisco Aironet is to:
   a. disable access to the WAP
   b. disable a router
   c. disable administrative access to the WAP
   d. disable security settings on the WAP

4. A recommended practice for wireless LANS is to:
   a. disable File and Print sharing
   b. disable NetBEUI
   c. enable WEP protection
   d. use a nonobvious encryption key
   e. all of the above

5. Which of the following can interfere with wireless transmission? (Choose all that apply.)
   a. brick walls
   b. cell phones
   c. cordless phones
   d. distance

LAB 8.4 ADDING ADMINISTRATIVE USERS TO THE AIRONET

Objectives

As discussed in Lab 8.3, you can add additional users with the Aironet User Manager. This is useful if you plan to log events, including configuration changes. One common mistake that companies make is to share the Administrator password with all administrators. This is not a good practice because you can never be sure which administrator has made changes to the configuration. Each administrator that is to have access to this device should use his or her own username and password, so that you can keep track of who is making changes.

After completing this lab, you will be able to:

➤ Allow users to access the Aironet Configuration

➤ Grant permissions to new users

Materials Required

This lab will require the following:

➤ A Windows 2000 server

➤ DHCP server

➤ A Cisco Aironet 340 WAP

Estimated completion time: **10–15 minutes**

ACTIVITY

1. Launch **Internet Explorer**.

2. Enter the IP address of the Aironet in the Address box and then press **Enter**.

3. Log on as Administrator.

4. Click the **Setup** link.

5. Under Services, click the **Security** link.

6. Click **User Information**.

7. Click the **Add New User** button.

8. Enter your name and pick a password.

9. Click the following boxes under the capability settings: **Write**, **Firmware**, and **Admin**, as shown in Figure 8-12.

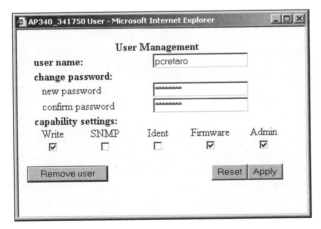

Figure 8-12   Properties for a new user account

10. Click **Apply**.

8

11. Close **Internet Explorer**.

12. Launch **Internet Explorer**.

13. Enter the IP address of the Aironet in the Address box and then press **Enter**.

14. Log in with your new account information.

15. Click **Setup**.

16. Under Services, click **Console/Telnet**.

17. Click the **Enabled** radio button.

18. Click **Apply**.

19. Click **Cancel** and close **Internet Explorer**.

Certification Objectives

Objectives for CompTIA Security+ Exam:

➤ Communication Security: Wireless

➤ Communication Security: Wireless: WEP/WAP

Review Questions

1. Administrators should use a separate account because it makes the system more secure. True or False?

2. Administrators should use separate account because it makes auditing easier and more reliable. True or False?

3. The Cisco Aironet application used to administer access is called:

   a. Server Manger

   b. User Manger

   c. Computer Management

   d. WAP Manager

4. Which of the following are capability settings available to user accounts? (Choose all that apply.)

   a. Write

   b. SNMP

   c. Firmware

   d. Admin

5. To enable User Manager at least one account must have full power. True or False?

LAB 8.5 RESTORING THE AIRONET FACTORY DEFAULT SETTINGS

Objectives

In this lab, you will restore the factory default settings to the Aironet to undo the changes made during the lab activities in this chapter. This is a good practice when you install a device out of the box, as you can never be sure if the box was opened then returned.

After completing this lab, you will be able to:

➤ Reset the Aironet settings to the factory defaults

➤ Undo the changes made to the Cisco Aironet during the performance of these lab exercises

Materials Required

This lab will require the following:

➤ A Windows 2000 Server

➤ DHCP server

➤ A Cisco Aironet 340 WAP

Estimated completion time: **15 minutes**

ACTIVITY

1. Launch **Internet Explorer**.

2. Enter the IP address of the Aironet in the Address box and then press **Enter**.

3. Log in as Administrator.

4. Click the **Setup** link.

5. Under Services, click the **Cisco Services** link, as shown in Figure 8-13.

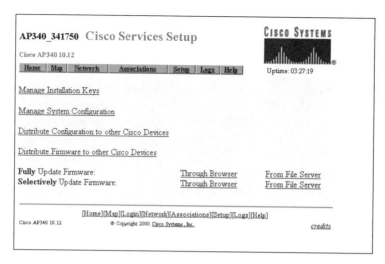

Figure 8-13   Aironet 340 Cisco Services Setup screen

6. Click the **Manage System Configuration** link, as shown in Figure 8-14.

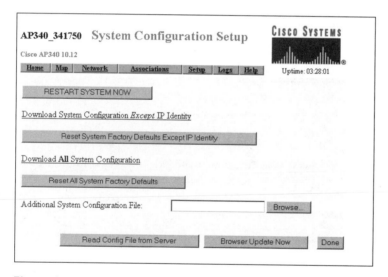

Figure 8-14   Aironet 340 System Configuration Setup screen

7. Click **Reset System Factory Defaults Except IP Identity**. Note: This will reset all devices, except for the IP address, and any accounts that you created.

8. You will receive the message shown in Figure 8-15.

Figure 8-15 Warning message

9. Click **OK**. You will receive the message shown in Figure 8-16.

A major change in the system's configuration has been performed, making a full restart of AP340_341750 necessary within 5 seconds. After 30 seconds, please click here to continue working from the page you were viewing previously, or click here to continue working from the Summary Status page.

Figure 8-16 Aironet settings have been reset message

10. Close **Internet Explorer**.

11. Launch **Internet Explorer**.

12. Enter the IP address of the Aironet in the Address box and then press **Enter**. Notice that you are still required to log in. Log on as Administrator.

13. You are now at the **Express Setup** menu, as shown in Figure 8-17.

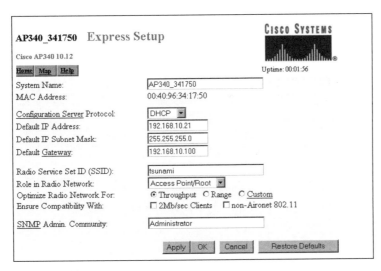

Figure 8-17 The Cisco Aironet 340 Express Setup screen

14. You are now ready to configure the Cisco Aironet.

Certification Objectives

Objectives for CompTIA Security+ Exam:

➤ Communication Security: Wireless

➤ Communication Security: Wireless: WEP/WAP

Review Questions

1. The 802.11a standard can use which of the following bands?
   a. 2.4GHz
   b. 5GHz
   c. 2.4 MHz
   d. 5MHz

2. The 802.11b standard uses which of the following bands?
   a. 2.4GH
   b. 5GHz
   c. 2.4 MHz
   d. 5MHz

3. The 802.11a standard can transmit data at speeds of up to
   _____ Mbps.
   a. 11
   b. 36
   c. 48
   d. 54

4. The 802.11b standard can transmit data at speeds of up to
   _____ Mbps.
   a. 11
   b. 36
   c. 48
   d. 54

5. Which of the following protocols is used to encrypt wireless transmission?
   a. WAP
   b. WEP
   c. WSP
   d. WDP

DEVICES

Labs included in this chapter:

➤ Lab 9.1 Installing Windows 2000, Service Packs, and Hotfixes

➤ Lab 9.2 Protecting the System Accounts Database

➤ Lab 9.3 Configuring Complex Passwords and Other Security Settings

➤ Lab 9.4 Configuring Services and Processes

➤ Lab 9.5 Configuring Network Settings

CompTIA Security+ Exam Objectives	
Objective	**Lab**
Infrastructure Security: Devices	9.1, 9.2, 9.3, 9.4, 9.5
Infrastructure Security: Security Baselines: Application Hardening	9.1, 9.2, 9.3, 9.4, 9.5

Lab 9.1 Installing Windows 2000, Service Packs, and Hotfixes

Objectives

Securing an operating system is an ongoing process. When an OS is released and it begins to be used by a large number of systems, many previously unknown security holes and bugs are routinely discovered. An OS has so many bugs due, primarily, to the complexity of the design behind each component. If you plan to use a software-based firewall such as Microsoft's ISA server or Checkpoint Firewall-1, it is very important that you "harden" the server prior to installing the firewall software. Once the hardening process is complete, the server is known as a bastion host. The first step to hardening a server is to apply the latest service pack and all patches and hotfixes. In this lab you will Install Windows 2000 Server and apply the latest service pack and patches.

After completing this lab, you will be able to:

➤ Install Windows 2000

➤ Apply Windows 2000 Service Packs, patches, and hotfixes

Materials Required

This lab will require the following:

➤ A Windows 2000 server

➤ A Windows 2000 Server CD

➤ Internet access

Estimated completion time: **60 minutes**

Activity

1. Log on to your server as Administrator.

2. Insert the Windows 2000 Server CD-ROM. Close the autorun window if it appears.

3. Click **Start**, **Run**, and click **Browse**. Navigate to your CD-ROM drive.

4. Double-click the **I386** folder.

5. Double-click **WINNT32.exe**.

6. Click **OK** to run the file. Click **Next** on the welcome screen, select **Clean Install**, and then click **Next**.

7. Click the **Advanced Options** button on the **Select Special Options** window, as shown in Figure 9-1.

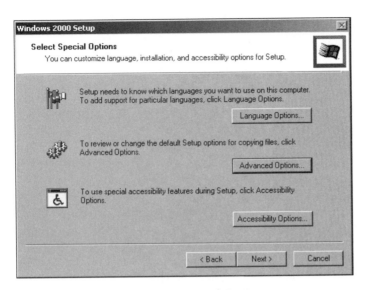

Figure 9-1   Windows 2000 Special Options

8. Change the Windows installation folder to **\Bastion**, as shown in Figure 9-2. Click **OK**.

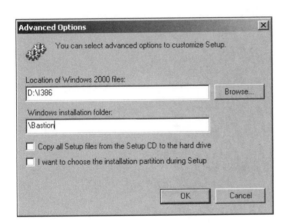

Figure 9-2   Windows 2000 Advanced Options

9. If you are prompted to upgrade to NTFS, select **Yes**, as shown in Figure 9-3, and click **Next**.

10. Click **Next** to skip the **Directory of Applications for Windows 2000 compatibility** window. Setup will copy files and restart.

11. The text-based Server setup will begin. Click **Enter**.

12. Press **Esc** when prompted to repair.

13. Choose the **C:** drive for the partition. If you are low on space you can choose another partition.

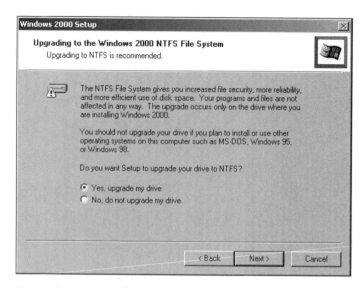

Figure 9-3   NTFS file system warning

14. Press **Enter** to select the partition.

15. Press **C** to continue. Setup will copy and install files, and then the computer will restart. The GUI portion will then run.

16. Click **Next**, and then click **Next** again to accept the Regional Settings.

17. Enter your name and organization and then click **Next**.

18. Click the **Per Seat Licensing Mode**, and then click **Next**.

19. For your computer name enter **BastionXXX** (where *XXX* is your student number). Enter **password** for your password.

20. Click **Next**.

21. Uncheck all of the boxes in Windows 2000 Components.

22. Click **Next**.

23. Adjust the date and time settings to your area.

24. Click the **Custom settings** radio button.

25. Click **Next**.

26. Uncheck all boxes except for the TCP/IP protocol.

27. Click **Next**. If you have a second NIC, uncheck all boxes except for the TCP/IP protocol.

28. Click **Next** to remain in a WORKGROUP. Windows will install components.

29. Click **Finish** once the Setup Wizard completes. The server will reboot.

30. Log on as Administrator and go to *http://www.microsoft.com/security*.

31. Download the latest Service Pack and hotfixes.

32. Install the Service Pack, being sure to accept the license agreements and archive the files.

33. Install any additional hotfixes.

34. Log off and shut down the server.

Certification Objectives

Objectives for CompTIA Security+ Exam:

➤ Infrastructure Security: Devices

➤ Infrastructure Security: Security Baselines: Application Hardening

Review Questions

1. A DMZ is a part of the network that sits between the Internet and your
   _____.

   a. ISP

   b. VPN

   c. internal network

   d. firewall

2. Where on your network is a bastion host usually located?

   a. external to the DMZ

   b. the private side of a DMZ

   c. the public side of the DMZ

   d. behind a protective firewall or router

3. A bastion host should not be a member of your private domain. True or False?

4. Which of the following is often located in a DMZ?

   a. Web Server

   b. FTP Server

   c. DNS Servers

   d. all of the above

5. The goal of using a bastion host is to _____.

   a. sacrifice a system

   b. prevent break-ins

   c. delay break-ins

   d. track break-in attempts

9

LAB 9.2 PROTECTING THE SYSTEM ACCOUNTS DATABASE

Objectives

If an intruder can gain physical access to a server, utilities such as LOphtCrack can be used to get a list of accounts and passwords. One way to prevent this is to encrypt the accounts database. Beginning with Windows NT SP3, Microsoft provides the syskey tool to encrypt the accounts database. Syskey will create a random 128-bit encryption key, which is then protected with the system key. This program also offers the option to store the key on a floppy disk, which requires that the floppy disk is inserted to start the system. While this makes a system very secure, it can also be dangerous because if the floppy disk is lost or corrupt, Windows will have to be reinstalled.

After completing this lab, you will be able to:

➤ Understand how to use the syskey command

➤ Change the location of the startup password

Materials Required

This lab will require the following:

➤ A hardened Windows 2000 server

➤ All of the latest Windows 2000 Service Packs and hotfixes

Estimated completion time: **15 minutes**

ACTIVITY

1. Log on to the bastion host as Administrator.
2. Change the Administrator password to **Pa$$word**.
3. Click **Start**, **Run**, and type **syskey**. Press **Enter**.
4. Notice in Figure 9-4 that the **Encryption Disabled** option is not available. Windows 2000 encrypts the accounts database by default.

Figure 9-4   Securing the Windows NT account database, with encryption enabled

5. Click the **Update** button.

6. Select the **Password Startup** radio button, as shown in Figure 9-5.

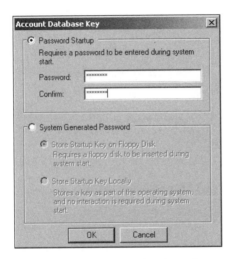

Figure 9-5   Account database key configuration window

7. Enter **password** as the password.

8. Click **OK**. You will be notified that the Account Database Startup Key was changed. Click **OK**.

9. Restart the server.

10. When the computer restarts you will be asked to enter the Startup password.

11. Log off Administrator.

Certification Objectives

Objectives for CompTIA Security+ Exam:

➤ Infrastructure Security: Devices

➤ Infrastructure Security: Security Baselines: Application Hardening

Review Questions

1. Which of the following is the file that contains the Windows accounts database?

   a. Accounts

   b. Secedit

   c. SAM

   d. SAM.dbf

2. If the system key is lost, it is impossible to recover the system. True or False?

3. Syskey encrypts which of the following registry hives? (Choose all that apply.)

   a. SOFTWARE

   b. SAM

   c. SYSTEM

   d. SECURITY

4. Which of the following are system security component files that are affected by syskey? (Choose all that apply.)

   a. Winlogon.exe

   b. SAM

   c. Samsrv.dll

   d. Samlib.dll

5. Which of the following methods are used by LOphtCrack to attack the accounts database? (Choose all that apply.)

   a. dictionary

   b. brute force

   c. random generated

   d. sniffing

LAB 9.3 CONFIGURING COMPLEX PASSWORDS AND OTHER SECURITY SETTINGS

Objectives

Password policies are very important in any networking environment. All nodes and devices on the network need to be protected from an intrusion, and passwords are the first line of defense. However, a weak password is almost as bad as no password at all. For example, all networking devices have default passwords that are readily available. Failure to change these passwords is a common and major mistake. Organizations without a full time IT staff are usually guilty of this. Creating a complex password requirement is one of the steps in creating a bastion host. The bastion.inf file has recommended security settings that can be applied using the secedit command.

After completing this lab, you will be able to:

➤ Modify the Windows 2000 Local Security Policy

➤ Change the password policy so that passwords must meet complexity requirements

Materials Required

This lab will require the following:

➤ A hardened Windows 2000 server

➤ All of the latest Service Packs and hotfixes

➤ A file named bastion.inf, available on the Student Downloads area of the Course Technology Web site (*www.course.com*)

Estimated completion time: **15–20 minutes**

ACTIVITY

1. Boot to the bastion host.

2. Enter **password** for the System Startup key.

3. Log on to the bastion server as Administrator.

4. Click **Start**, **Programs**, **Administrative Tools**, and select **Local Security Policy**.

5. Expand **Account Policies**.

6. Select **Password Policy**.

7. Double-click the **Passwords must meet complexity requirements** option.

8. Click the **Enabled** radio button.

9. Click **OK**.

10. Try to change the Administrator password to password. It will fail.

11. To lock down the rest of the Security settings you will need to apply the **bastion.inf** file.

12. Copy the **bastion.inf** to c:\. This file can be found in the Student Downloads area of the Course Technology Web site (*www.course.com*).

13. Click **Start**, **Run**, and type **cmd**. Press **Enter**.

14. Type the following in the command line: **Secedit /configure /cfg bastion.inf / db %temp%\secedit.sdb /verbose /log %temp%\seclog.txt**

15. The system will run through 162 items, some of which may not be on your server.

16. Look at the **seclog.txt** file to see the results. This file will be created automatically. Note: bastion.inf renames the Administrator account to root and disables the DHCP client.

9

Certification Objectives

Objectives for CompTIA Security+ Exam:

➤ Infrastructure Security: Devices

➤ Infrastructure Security: Security Baselines: Application Hardening

Review Questions

1. Which of the following authentication methods is used by Windows NT and 2000?

   a. IPSec

   b. NTLM

   c. Kerberos

   d. all of the above

2. The primary reason Windows passwords are weak is because of the simple password-hashing algorithm used. True or False?

3. NTLM uses which of the following processes to authenticate a user?

   a. reversible encryption

   b. challenge/response

   c. plaintext

   d. smart card

4. When you change the Windows 2000 password policies, they will take effect when _____.

   a. each PC is rebooted

   b. the Domain Controller is rebooted

   c. the current passwords expire

   d. Active Directory replicates

5. NTLM sends passwords across the network during the authentication process. True or False?

LAB 9.4 CONFIGURING SERVICES AND PROCESSES

Objectives

When creating a bastion host it is also important to remove all unnecessary or unused services and programs. These services and programs may be used to exploit a weakness in the operating system or simply consume system resources. Programs such as Telnet, ftp, and any editors should be removed. Services for NetBIOS and the spooler should also be removed. The idea behind this procedure is to run only what is necessary and remove any programs that are not needed. This can be one of the more difficult steps in creating a bastion host because of the size of the operating systems. Windows 2000 has twice as many services available as Windows NT, making it even more difficult to harden.

After completing this lab, you will be able to:

➤ Configure Services and Processes

➤ Disable unnecessary services

Materials Required:

This lab will require the following:

➤ A hardened Windows 2000 Server

➤ All of the latest Service Packs and hotfixes

Estimated completion time: **30–45 minutes**

ACTIVITY

1. Boot to the bastion host.

2. Enter **Password** for the System Startup key.

3. Log on to the bastion server as **Administrator**.

4. Click **Start**, **Programs**, **Administrative Tools**, and select **Services**.

5. To change the Service settings, double-click on the service for which you wish to change settings.

6. Configure the following Services to Start Automatically:

   - DNS Client
   - Event Log
   - Logical Disk Manager
   - Network Connections
   - Plug and Play
   - Protected Storage
   - Remote Procedure Call (RPC)
   - RunAs Service
   - Security Accounts Manager
   - Task Scheduler
   - Windows Management Instrumentation
   - Windows Management Instrumentation Driver Extensions

9

7. Configure the **Logical Disk Manager Administrative Service** to start manually.

8. Disable all other services. (Note: If you use DHCP, enable the DHCP client at this time.)

9. Log off Administrator.

Certification Objectives

Objectives for CompTIA Security+ Exam:

➤ Infrastructure Security: Devices

➤ Infrastructure Security: Security Baselines: Application Hardening

Review Questions

1. Which of the following terms best describes a service that depends on another service to function properly?

   a. required

   b. dependency

   c. child

   d. parent

2. Which of the following is a valid startup type for services?

   a. manual

   b. automatic

   c. disabled

   d. all of the above

3. Services authenticate by using the users account and password. True or False?

4. Which of the following is the equivalent to stopping and starting a service?

   a. restart

   b. reset

   c. redo

   d. reboot

5. Which of the following services supports pass-through authentication for computers in a domain?

   a. Winlogon

   b. Workstation

   c. Net Logon

   d. Server

LAB 9.5 CONFIGURING NETWORK SETTINGS

Objectives

Once the operating system services and programs are hardened it is necessary to restrict network access to the server. Most intrusion attempts will take place over a network connection. These intrusions are not limited to remote users and hackers. The local network can also be used to exploit a weakness. During this lab, you will lock down TCP/IP and remove any unnecessary protocols.

After completing this lab, you will be able to:

➤ Configure advanced network settings

➤ Configure TCP/IP filters

Materials Required

This lab will require the following:

➤ A hardened Windows 2000 server

➤ All of the latest Service Packs and hotfixes

Estimated completion time: **15–30 minutes**

ACTIVITY

1. Boot to the bastion host.

2. Enter **Password** for the System Startup key.

3. Log on to the bastion server as **Administrator**.

4. Right-click **My Computer** and select **Properties**.

5. Select the **Hardware** tab, as shown in Figure 9-6.

6. Click the **Device Manager** button. You will see a screen similar to the one shown in Figure 9-7.

7. Click **View**, **Show hidden devices**.

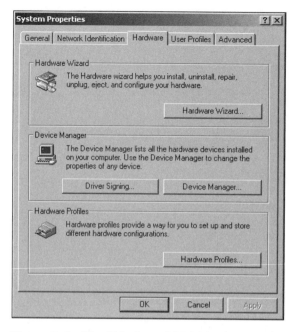

Figure 9-6   The Windows 2000 Hardware tab

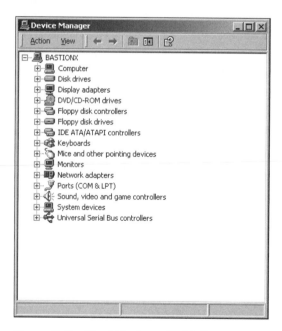

Figure 9-7   The Windows 2000 Device Manager

8. Expand **Non-Plug and Play Drivers**, as shown in Figure 9-8.

9. Right-click **NetBIOS over Tcpip**, and select **Uninstall**.

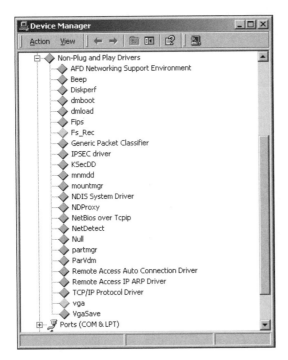

Figure 9-8   Non-Plug and Play Drivers

10. Click **OK** and reboot.

11. Right-click **My Network Places** and select **Properties**.

12. Right-click your **Local Area Connection**, then select **Properties**.

13. Double-click **Internet Protocol (TCP/IP)**.

14. Click the **Advanced** button.

15. Select the **WINS** tab.

16. Click the **Disable NetBIOS over TCP/IP** radio button, as shown in Figure 9-9.

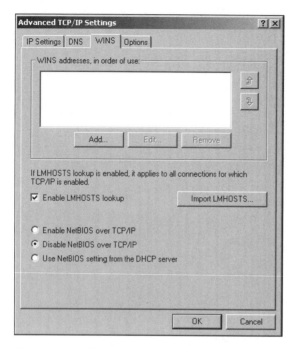

Figure 9-9   Disabling NetBIOS over TCP/IP

17. Click **OK** three times.

18. Repeat this process for all network cards.

19. NetBIOS is now disabled on this server. To test this, have the instructor disable DNS, and ping another server in the room using only the computer name. It will fail.

20. Ping the same server using the ip address and you will be successful.

The preceding labs are meant to be a general guide for creating a bastion host. In a production environment you may have to take further steps to protect the server. Normally, you would not use a dual boot on a true bastion host; this was done for lab functionality only.

Certification Objectives

Objectives for CompTIA Security+ Exam:

➤ Infrastructure Security: Devices

➤ Infrastructure Security: Security Baselines: Application Hardening

Review Questions

1. Which of the following is a broadcast-based protocol?

   a. TCP

   b. UDP

   c. NetBIOS

   d. IP

2. In Windows 2000, it is possible to filter which of the following protocols? (Choose all that apply.)

   a. TCP

   b. UDP

   c. NetBIOS

   d. IP

3. In Windows 2000, which of the following options are available to filter? (Choose all that apply.)

   a. Permit All

   b. Deny All

   c. Permit Only

   d. Deny Only

4. Windows 2000 offers another level of TCP/IP protection by supporting which of the following?

   a. PGP

   b. IPSec

   c. EFS

   d. MD5

5. To configure TCP/IP filtering you will need to know which of the following? (Choose all that apply.)

   a. protocol

   b. port

   c. IP address

   d. network ID

MEDIA

Labs included in this chapter:

➤ Lab 10.1 Transferring NTFS Encrypted Files

➤ Lab 10.2 Installing and Running LSoft ZDelete Auto-Cleaner and Bitmart Restorer2000

➤ Lab 10.3 Using ZDelete Auto-Cleaner – Disk Wiper

➤ Lab 10.4 Installing Microsoft Network Monitor

➤ Lab 10.5 Using Microsoft Network Monitor to Sniff an FTP Session

CompTIA Security+ Exam Objectives	
Objective	Lab
Infrastructure Security: Media	10.1, 10.2, 10.3, 10.4, 10.5

LAB 10.1 TRANSFERRING NTFS ENCRYPTED FILES

Objectives

An advanced feature of NTFS is the ability to encrypt files and folders. Unlike most encryption programs, NTFS encryption is transparent to the user. This is especially useful for users that are not concerned with learning the details behind the operating system, but who want to create data, encrypt it, and move on. The disadvantage to transparent encryption, however, is that while the users are not bothered by knowing which data is encrypted, they also are not notified about which data is decrypted, opening a potential security hole.

After completing this lab, you will be able to:

> ➤ Encrypt a file on an NTFS partition

> ➤ Remove the encryption by copying the file to a floppy disk

Materials Required

This lab will require the following:

> ➤ A Windows 2000 server with an NTFS partition

> ➤ A floppy disk

Estimated completion time: **10–15 minutes**

ACTIVITY

1. Log on to your server as Administrator.

2. Right-click **My Computer** and select **Explore**.

3. Navigate to **C:\Documents and Settings\Administrator**.

4. Right-click the **Start** menu and select **Properties**.

5. Click the **Advanced** button.

6. Check the **Encrypt contents to secure data** box, as shown in Figure 10-1.

7. Click **OK**.

8. Click **OK**; you will be asked to confirm changes.

9. Click the **Apply changes to this folder, subfolders and files** radio button, as shown in Figure 10-2.

10. Click **OK**.

11. Right-click **Start** menu and select **Send To, 3½ Floppy (A:)**.

12. Once the files are copied, navigate to the floppy disk drive.

Figure 10-1   Advanced Attributes used to configure NTFS encryption

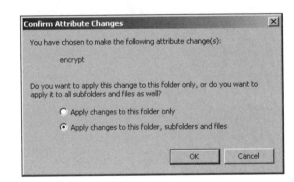

10

Figure 10-2   The Confirm Attribute Changes dialog box

13. Right-click the **Start** menu, and select **Properties**. You will see a screen resembling the one shown in Figure 10-3. Notice that the Advanced button is no longer available. The files were decrypted.

Certification Objectives

Objectives for CompTIA Security+ Exam:

➤ Infrastructure Security: Media

Review Questions

1. Which versions of Windows Support NTFS Encryption?

a. Windows 2000

b. Windows XP

c. Windows NT 4 SP4

d. all of the above

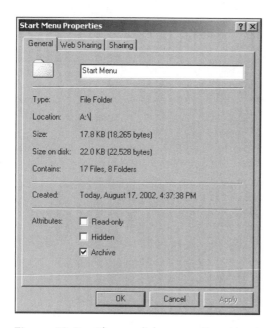

Figure 10-3   Floppy disk properties showing that encryption was removed

2. A file will retain its encryption status if:

   a. it is copied to a floppy disk

   b. it is compressed, then copied to a floppy disk

   c. it is copied to an NTFS partition

   d. it is copied to a FAT partition

3. Which of the following accounts can recover encrypted files?

   a. the owner

   b. administrator

   c. recovery agent

   d. all of the above

4. If a disgruntled user deletes his keys before leaving a job, the administrator may log on as the user to decrypt the files. True or False?

5. If you attempt to encrypt a compressed folder, what will happen?

   a. The compression will remain.

   b. The compression will be removed.

   c. The encryption will be denied.

   d. The process will be denied.

LAB 10.2 INSTALLING AND RUNNING LSOFT ZDELETE AUTO-CLEANER AND BITMART RESTORER2000

Objectives

When a file is deleted in Windows 2000 the operating system places it in the Recycle Bin. This essentially just removes the file from the directory listing, but the space on the disk is still reserved. Once the Recycle Bin is emptied, the file is removed from the file allocation table (FAT partitions) or master file table (NTFS partitions) and the first character is deleted. However, the file still exists on the hard drive until the space is overwritten by another file or by the defragmentation process. Files that have been recently deleted can easily be recovered with the appropriate tools, such as Norton Utilities. Programs such as ZDelete were created to protect the privacy of confidential data. ZDelete can permanently erase data using a process that actually overwrites the deleted files with random 1s and 0s, making the file impossible to recover. Otherwise, programs such as Restorer2000 can be used to restore deleted files.

After completing this lab, you will be able to:

➤ Install and configure LSoft Technologies ZDelete program

➤ Install the Bitmart Inc. Restorer2000 program

10

Materials Required

This lab will require the following:

➤ A Windows 2000 server

➤ The LSoft Technologies ZDelete program, available on the Web at *www.zdelete.com*

➤ The Bitmart Inc. Restorer2000 program, available on the Web at *www.bitmart.net*

Estimated completion time: **30 minutes**

ACTIVITY

1. Download a free version of ZDelete.

2. Launch the **ZDeleteSetup.exe** setup file. Click **Next**.

3. Select the **I Agree to the terms of the license** radio button, and click **Next**.

4. Click **Next** to accept the default installation location, as shown in Figure 10-4.

5. Select the **Program Files** and **Help** components to install, as shown in Figure 10-5. Click **Next**.

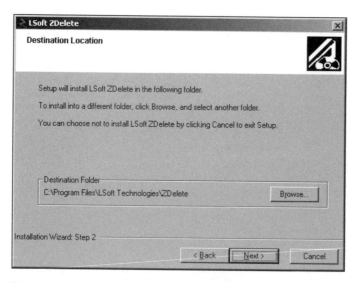

Figure 10-4   ZDelete destination location

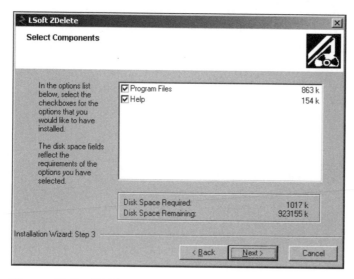

Figure 10-5   ZDelete component selection

6. Click **Next** to start the installation.

7. Once the files are copied, check the **Run ZDelete Wizard to configure software** box and click **Finish**. The configuration Wizard will start.

8. Click **Next**.

9. Accept the default settings in Step 2 and click **Next**.

10. Click **Next** for Step 3, not selecting any Custom Items.

11. Click **Next** to skip Step 4.

12. Click **Finish** to accept all default options, as shown in Figure 10-6.

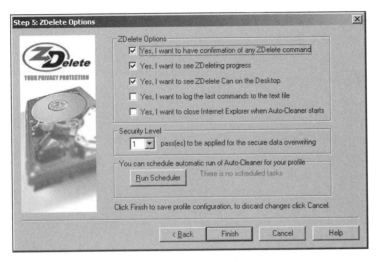

Figure 10-6   ZDelete Wizard step 5: ZDelete options

10

13. Close all windows.

14. Launch Restorer2000 by double-clicking **r2k_demo.exe**.

15. Check the **I agree with the above terms and conditions** box and click **Next**.

16. Click **Start** to accept the default installation location.

17. Uncheck the **Run Installed Application** box, as shown in Figure 10-7.

Figure 10-7   Restorer2000 installation complete screen

18. Click **OK**.

19. Close all windows and log off.

Certification Objectives

Objectives for CompTIA Security+ Exam:

➤ Infrastructure Security: Media

Review Questions

1. The NTFS MFT is created when an NTFS volume is formatted. True or False?

2. Which of the following commands can be entered to determine the size of the MFT in Windows NT?

   a. dir $mft

   b. dir /a $mft

   c. dir /s $mft

   d. use a disk defragmenter

3. Which of the following commands can be entered to determine the size of the MFT in Windows 2000?

   a. dir $mft

   b. dir /a $mft

   c. dir /s $mft

   d. use a disk defragmenter

4. When you empty the Recycle Bin you cannot recover the files without a special utility. True or False?

5. If you wish to delete a file without sending it to the Recycle Bin, you must hold the _____ key down while deleting.

   a. Shift

   b. Ctrl

   c. Alt

   d. F10

LAB 10.3 USING ZDELETE AUTO-CLEANER – DISK WIPER

Objectives

Occasionally in an organization, sensitive information needs to be stored somewhere other than the network, to prevent any unauthorized access. In these cases, external media are used to store the information. The most common media used in this situation are the floppy disk for small files and the zip disk for larger files. There may be times when a disk has to be wiped clean. While you may wish to destroy the disk, another more economical method is to use a disk cleaning software application such as ZDelete's Disk Wiper. Once files have been wiped clean by ZDelete's Disk Wiper, programs such as Restorer2000 will be unable to recover the files.

After completing this lab, you will be able to:

➤ Use Restorer2000 to recover deleted files

➤ Use ZDelete – Disk Wiper to completely erase files

Materials Required

This lab will require the following:

➤ A Windows 2000 server

➤ ZDelete-Disk Wiper

➤ Restorer2000

Estimated completion time: **25–30 minutes**

10

ACTIVITY

1. Log on as Administrator.

2. Right-click **My Computer** and select **Explore**.

3. Create three folders on the root directory of your hard drive (C:) named **Recoverable**, **Unrecoverable**, and **restore**.

4. Create a text file named **YourNameRecoverable.txt** (replacing YourName with your name).

5. Copy the file to the **Recoverable** folder.

6. Create a text file named **YourNameUnrecoverable.txt** (replacing YourName with your name).

7. Copy the file to the **Unrecoverable** folder.

8. Delete the file in the **Recoverable** folder.

9. Empty the Recycle Bin.

10. Click **Start**, **Programs**, **Restorer2000 Demo**, **Restorer2000 Demo**. You will see a screen resembling the one shown in Figure 10-8.

11. Right-click **c:** and select **Open Drive Files F5**.

12. Expand **Root** and navigate to the **RECYCLER** folder. This folder is created automatically by the Restorer2000 program.

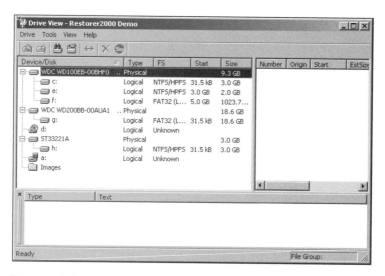

Figure 10-8   Restorer2000 drive view screen

13. Expand the folders until you find the text file you deleted in Step 8. Make a note of the new folder name. It should be De1, as the names are listed in numerical order. This name may vary, and will depend on what you have already deleted.

14. Right–click the folder that contains your text file, and select **Recover... F2**.

15. Enter **c:\restore** in the **Output** folder, as shown in Figure 10-9.

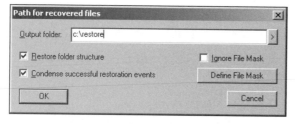

Figure 10-9   Alternate path to recover files

16. Uncheck the **Ignore File Mask** box, if necessary, and then click **OK**. You will receive the warning shown in Figure 10-10.

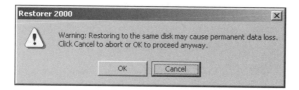

Figure 10-10   Warning message about restoring to the original location

17. Click **OK**.

18. Once the recovery is complete, close Restorer2000 and navigate to the **restore** folder to find your file.

19. Navigate to the **Unrecoverable** folder and delete it.

20. Empty the Recycle Bin.

21. Double-click **My Computer** and navigate to the **RECYCLER** folder.

22. Right-click the **RECYCLER** folder and select **ZDelete**.

23. Click **Next**.

24. Make sure My Recycle Bin is the only box checked. Click **Yes**.

25. When the program finishes, close all windows.

26. Click **Start**, **Programs**, **Restorer2000 Demo**, **Restorer2000 Demo**.

27. Right-click **c:** and select **Open Drive Files F5**.

28. Expand **Root** and navigate to the **RECYCLER** folder. Notice that the **YourNameUnrecoverable.txt** file is not recoverable.

29. Close all windows and log off.

Certification Objectives

Objectives for CompTIA Security+ Exam:

➤ Infrastructure Security: Media

Review Questions

1. When you delete a file, the system simply takes the first bit of the file and replaces it with another bit. True or False?

2. Most files do not fully utilize the clusters allocated to them. This leftover space that may still contain old data is known as:

   a. free space

   b. MFT space

   c. slack space

   d. leftover space

3. A file wiper will overwrite areas not allocated with random data to prevent recovery. True or False?

4. Which of the following methods is the only true way to guarantee data has been deleted?

   a. Empty the Recycle Bin.

   b. Destroy the hardware and all backups.

   c. FDISK the hard drive.

   d. Format the hard drive and then burn it.

5. Which of the following are methods of data recovery after a disk has been wiped? (Choose all that apply.)

   a. CD-ROM archives

   b. backup tapes

   c. e-mail

   d. none of the above

LAB 10.4 INSTALLING MICROSOFT NETWORK MONITOR

Objectives

Network Monitor is provided with Windows 2000 and offers basic network sniffing features. It is a good learning tool, but it is limited to sniffing packets from the local NIC. Microsoft also offers an enhanced version of Network Monitor that can operate in promiscuous mode and sniff packets from any computer on the network. This product should be used on a production network and is packaged along with Microsoft Systems Management Server.

After completing this lab, you will be able to:

➤ Install Network Monitor

➤ Configure Network Monitor to operate on the appropriate NIC

Materials Required

This lab will require the following:

➤ A Windows 2000 server

➤ A Windows 2000 installation CD-ROM

➤ Access to the network interface card on your classroom network

Estimated completion time: **10–15 minutes**

ACTIVITY

1. Log on as Administrator.

2. Click **Start**, **Settings**, **Control Panel**.

3. Double-click **Add/Remove Programs**.

4. Click **Add/Remove Windows Components**.

5. Highlight **Management and Monitoring Tools**, and then click **Details**.

6. Check the **Network Monitor Tools** box, and click **OK**.

7. Click **Next**. If prompted, insert the Windows 2000 Server CD, and then click **OK**.

8. Click **Finish**.

9. Click **Close** to close the **Add/Remove Programs** window.

10. Close the Control Panel window.

11. Click **Start Run**, and type **cmd**. Press **Enter**.

12. In the command line, type **ipconfig /all**, press **Enter**, and write down the MAC address of the network card that is on the classroom network.

13. Click **Start**, **Programs**, **Administrative Tools**, and then select **Network Monitor**.

14. You will receive the message shown in Figure 10–11.

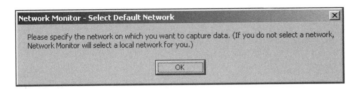

Figure 10-11   Network Monitor default network selection warning

15. Click **OK**.

16. Expand **Local Computer** and select the appropriate NIC (the MAC address you wrote down in Step 12). The screen will resemble the one shown in Figure 10–12. Click **OK**.

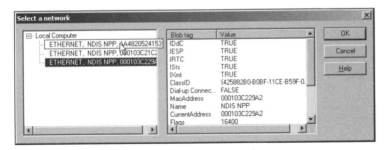

Figure 10-12   Choosing the NIC with the correct MAC address

17. Close all windows and log off.

Certification Objectives

Objectives for CompTIA Security+ Exam:

➤ Infrastructure Security: Media

Review Questions

1. By default, Network Monitor will capture all data sent to your NIC. What can be used to narrow the scope of the data collected?

   a. a NIC in promiscuous mode

   b. a screen

   c. a filter

   d. a strainer

2. Network Monitor is considered a sniffer. Which of the following is a characteristic of a sniffer?

   a. logging

   b. fault analysis

   c. performance analysis

   d. all of the above

3. Which Layer 2 device can limit the functionality of sniffing?

   a. a bridge

   b. a hub

   c. a switch

   d. a brouter

4. A packet is at which Layer of the OSI Model?

   a. Physical

   b. Data Link MAC

   c. Data Link LLC

   d. Network

5. A sniffer can be dangerous because it is very difficult to detect and can be attached to almost any part of a network. True or False?

LAB 10.5 USING MICROSOFT NETWORK MONITOR TO SNIFF AN FTP SESSION

Objectives

While Network Monitor is a very useful networking utility, it can also be used maliciously. As we discussed previously, FTP and Telnet send usernames and passwords in clear text. Network Monitor can capture the entire FTP session and present the username and password to the potential hacker. One way to prevent this is to use only anonymous access for FTP sites. Unfortunately, this does not enable you to lock down access to the server.

You could also configure the FTP server to only allow certain IP addresses or use a VPN connection to limit the access to the appropriate users.

After completing this lab, you will be able to:

➤ Capture an FTP session using Network Monitor

➤ Interpret the capture data to determine the username and password used

Materials Required

This lab will require the following:

➤ Two Windows 2000 servers with the FTP server service and Network Monitor installed

Estimated completion time: **15–30 minutes**

ACTIVITY

1. On Server-X, log on as Administrator.

2. Right-click **My Computer** and select **Manage**.

3. Expand **Services and Applications**.

4. Expand **Internet Information Services**; make sure the **Default FTP Site** is started.

5. Click **Start**, **Programs**, **Administrative Tools**, and select **Network Monitor**.

6. On the Menu bar click **Capture**, and then click **Start**.

7. On Server-Y, log on as Administrator.

8. Click **Start**, **Run**, and then type **cmd**. Press **Enter**.

9. Type **ftp server-x**. Note: You may also use the IP address of Server-X.

10. Enter **Administrator** for the user.

11. Enter **password** for the password.

12. Once you are logged on, type **quit**.

13. On Server-x, in the Network Monitor, click **Capture**, **Stop**, and then click **View**.

14. Examine frames 17 and 20 in Figure 10-13. The user account and password are listed. Note that the frame numbers may be different on your capture, but the frames containing the user account and password will be present.

15. Close all windows and log off on Server-X and Server-Y.

10

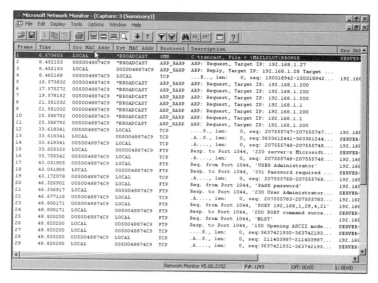

Figure 10-13   Network Monitor capture of an FTP session

Certification Objectives

Objectives for CompTIA Security+ Exam:

➤ Infrastructure Security: Media

Review Questions

1. Network Monitor captures and displays which of the following?

   a. source address

   b. destination address

   c. protocol

   d. data

   e. all of the above

2. Which of the following security features is available for the Full version of Network Monitor?

   a. Identify Network Monitor Users

   b. Intrusion detection system add-on

   c. Packet modification tools

   d. Password sniffing tools

3. Network Monitor will allow you to view encrypted data in plain text. True or False?

4. Which of the following protocols sends passwords and data in clear text?

   a. Telnet

   b. FTP

   c. HTTP

   d. NNTP

   e. IMAP

   f. POP

   g. SNMP

   h. all of the above

5. Which of the following protocols can be use to encrypt mail? (Choose all that apply.)

   a. PCP

   b. PGP

   c. MIME

   d. S/MIME

10

CHAPTER ELEVEN

NETWORK SECURITY TOPOLOGIES

Labs included in this chapter:

➤ Lab 11.1 Installing RRAS and NAT

➤ Lab 11.2 Configuring a Client to Access the Internet

➤ Lab 11.3 Configuring Output Filters to Block Internet Access

➤ Lab 11.4 Configuring Input Filters to Block Local FTP Access

➤ Lab 11.5 Configuring a VLAN

CompTIA Security+ Exam Objectives	
Objective	Lab
Infrastructure Security: Security Topologies	11.1, 11.2, 11.3, 11.4, 11.5
Infrastructure Security: Security Topologies: VLANs	11.5
Infrastructure Security: Security Topologies: NAT	11.1

LAB 11.1 INSTALLING RRAS AND NAT

Objectives

Windows 2000 Server Routing and Remote Access (RRAS) includes a service that can perform network address translation (NAT). NAT enables companies to connect their local area network to the Internet through a single connection. This method of connecting to the Internet conserves public IP addresses and can save companies money by requiring that they purchase fewer addresses. While NAT is not a firewall product, it does offer an additional layer of protection for the LAN. The NAT server acts as an intermediary, making all Internet requests for the clients. NAT operates similar to proxy servers, but unlike the proxy servers that operate at the transport and application layers of the OSI model, NAT operates at the network layer. Proxy servers can filter based on the content of the request; NAT can only filter based on network layer protocols. In this lab, you will learn how to configure RRAS, and its appropriate NAT settings.

After completing this lab, you will be able to:

➤ Configure Windows 2000 RRAS

➤ Configure NAT settings in RRAS

Materials Required

This lab will require the following:

➤ Two Windows 2000 servers

➤ A Windows 2000 Server CD

➤ Internet access

➤ A crossover cable

Estimated completion time: **60 minutes**

ACTIVITY

The servers used in this activity will be referred to as Server-X and Server-Y. Please substitute the names of your servers for these names.

1. On Server-X, log on as Administrator.

2. Click **Start**, **Programs**, **Administrative Tools**, **Routing and Remote Access**.

3. Right-click **Server-X** and select **Configure and Enable Routing and Remote Access**. The Routing and Remote Access Server Setup Wizard will begin.

4. Click **Next**.

5. Select **Internet connection server**, as shown in Figure 11-1.

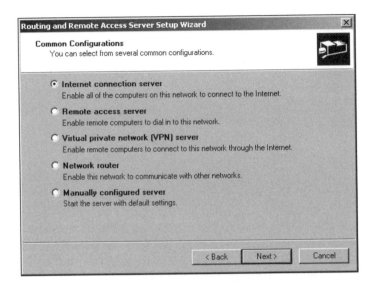

Figure 11-1   Routing and Remote Access Server Setup Wizard

6. Click **Next**.

7. Select **Set up a router with the Network Address Translation (NAT) routing protocol**, as shown in Figure 11-2.

11

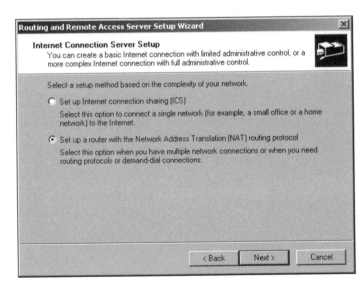

Figure 11-2   Choosing between Internet Connection Sharing and NAT

8. Click **Next**.

9. Select **Use the selected Internet connection**. Notice the two network cards, as shown in Figure 11-3. The External card should be connected to the classroom network and the Internal should be connected to Server-Y with a crossover cable.

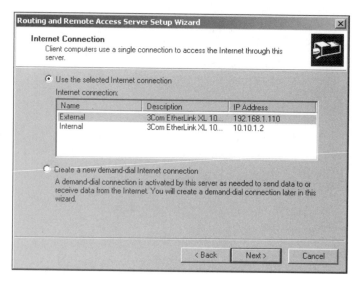

Figure 11-3   Choosing the Internet interface

10. Click **Next**.

11. Click **Finish**. Routing and Remote Access will start.

12. Expand Server-X, and then expand **IP Routing** and click **Network Address Translation (NAT)**, as shown in Figure 11-4.

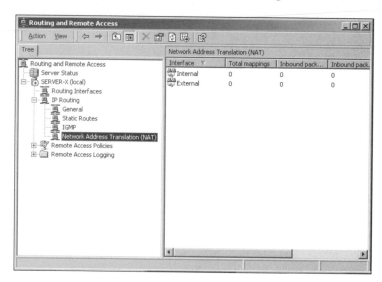

Figure 11-4   Interfaces used by NAT

13. Right-click the **Internal NIC** and select **Properties**.

14. Verify that the **Private interface connected to private network** radio button is selected, as shown in Figure 11-5.

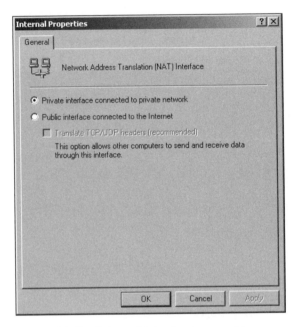

Figure 11-5   Internal interface properties

15. Click **OK**.

16. Right-click the **External** NIC and select **Properties**.

17. Verify that the **Public interface connected to the Internet** radio button is selected and that the **Translate TCP/UDP headers (recommended)** box is checked, as shown in Figure 11-6.

11

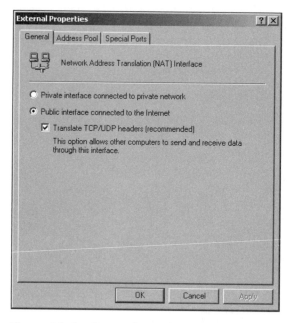

Figure 11-6   External interface properties

18. Click **OK**.

19. Close **Routing and Remote Access**.

20. Log off Administrator.

Certification Objectives

Objectives for CompTIA Security+ Exam:

➤ Infrastructure Security: Security Topologies: NAT

Review Questions

1. Which of the following protocols maps unregistered IP addresses to registered IP addresses on a one-to-one basis?

   a. dynamic NAT

   b. static NAT

   c. firewall NAT

   d. dynamic PAT

2. Which of the following IP address ranges is reserved for private networks?

   a. 10.0.0.0 through 10.255.255.255

   b. 172.16.0.0 through 172.31.255.255

   c. 192.168.0.0 through 192.168.255.255

   d. all of the above

3. An advantage that NAT has over Internet Connection Sharing is that it:

   a. can have multiple external IP addresses

   b. can have multiple internal IP addresses

   c. cannot have multiple external IP addresses

   d. cannot have multiple internal IP addresses

4. Which of the following is a form of dynamic NAT that maps multiple unregistered IP addresses to a single registered IP address by using different ports?

   a. overlapping

   b. overloading

   c. multiplexing

   d. mapping

5. On a server running Windows 2000 Routing and Remote Access with NAT, which interface should act as the default gateway for the local network?

   a. the external interface of the NAT server

   b. any interface on the NAT server

   c. the internal interface of the NAT server

   d. the internal interface of the local router

11

LAB 11.2 CONFIGURING A CLIENT TO ACCESS THE INTERNET

Objectives

Once the NAT server is properly configured you can begin to allow clients to access the Internet. If your network is using DHCP, this task can be completed without making any changes to the client. If you are not using DHCP, you will need the following: a valid IP address, a DNS server, and a default gateway. The default gateway will be the NAT server's IP address. Also note that if you are behind a proxy server you may have to configure the Internet Explorer settings to use a proxy server and a special port to be able to access the Internet. In this lab you will configure Internet access for a client.

After completing this lab, you will be able to:

➤ Configure a client to access the Internet using NAT

➤ Configure Network Property settings

Materials Required

This lab will require the following:

➤ A Windows 2000 server running RRAS with NAT

➤ A second Windows 2000 server to act as a client

➤ Internet access

➤ A crossover cable

> Estimated completion time: **15 minutes**

ACTIVITY

The servers used in this activity will be referred to as Server-X and Server-Y. Please substitute the names of your servers for these names.

1. On Server-Y, disconnect the cable connected to the classroom network.
2. Connect a crossover cable from Server-Y to Server-X.
3. Log on to Server-Y as Administrator.
4. Right-click **My Network Places** and select **Properties**.
5. Right-click the NIC connected to the classroom network and select **Disable**.
6. Right-click the NIC connected to Server-X and select **Properties**.
7. Highlight **Internet Protocol (TCP/IP)**.
8. Click **Properties**.
9. Verify that your IP address is on the same network as Server-X.
10. Verify that the Subnet mask is identical to Server-X.
11. Verify that the Default gateway is the IP address of the Internal NIC of Server-X.
12. Verify that the DNS server is the preferred IP address of the Instructor PC.
13. Click **OK** to close the Internet Protocol (TCP/IP) Properties.
14. Click **OK** to close the NIC Properties.
15. Open Internet Explorer to access the Internet. Navigate to your favorite Web site.
16. Log off Administrator.

Certification Objectives

Objectives for CompTIA Security+ Exam:

➤ Infrastructure Security: Security Topologies

Review Questions

1. A client that uses a NAT server to access the Internet is protected from Internet hackers. True or False?

2. Which of the following is the range of registered TCP/UDP ports?
   a. 0–1023
   b. 1024–49151
   c. 49152–65535
   d. all of the above

3. Which of the following is the range of dynamic TCP/UDP ports?

   a. 0–1023

   b. 1024–49151

   c. 49152–65535

   d. all of the above

4. Which of the following is the range of Well-Known TCP/UDP ports?

   a. 0–1023

   b. 1024–49151

   c. 49152–65535

   d. all of the above

5. One major difference between a proxy server and NAT is that:

   a. Proxy servers are transparent to the source PC, while NAT is not.

   b. Proxy servers are not transparent to the source PC, while NAT is.

   c. Proxy servers are not transparent to the destination, while NAT is.

   d. Proxy servers are transparent to the destination, while NAT is not.

LAB 11.3 CONFIGURING OUTPUT FILTERS TO BLOCK INTERNET ACCESS   11

Objectives

In some cases you may want to disable access to specific ports on the NAT server. For example, some companies have had users abuse Internet access by using it for non job-related tasks, such as listening to online radio stations. This may seem harmless to the average user, but it can be a nightmare for network engineers. The bandwidth consumption used by the Internet radio stations is very large and can get much worse if they are sending streaming video. Windows 2000 Server with RRAS has the ability to block specific ports to allow network engineers to manage Internet access. In this lab you will block Internet access.

After completing this lab, you will be able to:

➤ Configure NAT output filters

➤ Block Internet access for all users that use NAT

Materials Required

This lab will require the following:

➤ A Windows 2000 server running RRAS and NAT

➤ A second Windows 2000 server to act as a client

Estimated completion time: **15–20 minutes**

ACTIVITY

The servers used in this activity will be referred to as Server-X and Server-Y. Please substitute the names of your servers for these names.

1. Log on to Server-X as Administrator.

2. Click **Start**, **Programs**, **Administrative Tools**, **Routing and Remote Access**.

3. Expand **IP Routing** and click **General**, as shown in Figure 11-7.

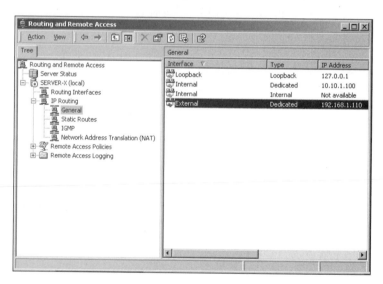

Figure 11-7   IP Routing general settings

4. Right-click the **External** NIC and select **Properties**. You will see a screen similar to the one shown in Figure 11-8.

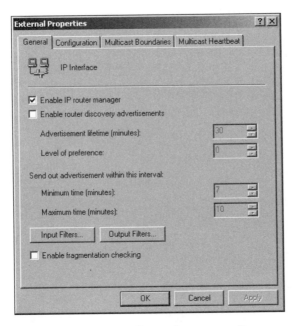

Figure 11-8   External interface properties

5. Click **Output Filters**. You will see a screen similar to the one shown in Figure 11–9.

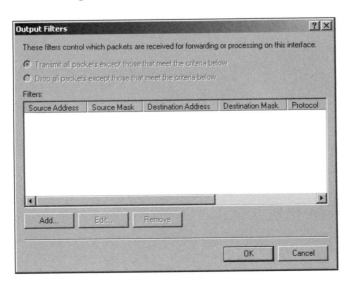

Figure 11-9   Output filters default settings

6. Click **Add**.

7. Enter the information shown in Figure 11–10.

Figure 11-10   Creating a Web input filter

8. Click **OK**.

9. Select the **Transmit all packets except those that meet the criteria below** radio button, as shown in Figure 11-11.

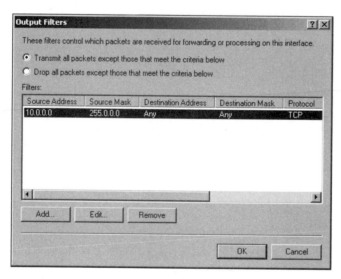

Figure 11-11   An applied input filter

10. Click **OK**.

11. Click **OK**.

12. Log on to Server-Y as Administrator.

13. Launch Internet Explorer. The Status bar will say "Web site Found. Waiting for reply...", but the page will never load.

14. After a few minutes you will receive the error message: "The page cannot be displayed".

15. Close all windows and log off.

Certification Objectives

Objectives for CompTIA Security+ Exam:

➤ Infrastructure Security: Security Topologies

Review Questions

1. To specify all destination networks enter _____ into the destination field.

   a. 0.0.0.0

   b. 255.255.255.255

   c. 254.254.254.254

   d. all of the above

2. Which of the following would filter the entire 10.0.0.0 network?

   a. 0.0.0.0

   b. 10.0.0.0

   c. 10.255.255.255

   d. 255.255.255.255

3. When filtering using RRAS, which of the following are options? (Choose all that apply.)

   a. Drop

   b. Reject

   c. Allow

   d. Receive

4. Which of the following protocols are necessary for allowing DNS traffic? (Choose all that apply.)

   a. TCP 53

   b. TCP 80

   c. UDP 53

   d. UDP 80

11

5. Output filters should be applied to which interface?

a. Internal

b. External

c. Both

LAB 11.4 CONFIGURING INPUT FILTERS TO BLOCK LOCAL FTP ACCESS

Objectives

FTP is a useful tool for transferring files across the Internet, but it has a major security flaw: it sends usernames and passwords across the LAN in plain text. By using Windows 2000 RRAS input and output filters, you can control FTP access without blocking other services. In this lab, you will block local FTP access but allow Internet FTP access. The reason for doing this is that local FTP traffic is susceptible to sniffing, while most Internet FTP sites use anonymous access, which is not.

After completing this lab, you will be able to:

➤ Configure NAT input filters

➤ Block local FTP access, but allow external FTP access

➤ Remove NAT input filters

Materials Required:

This lab will require the following:

➤ A Windows 2000 server running RRAS and NAT

➤ A Windows 2000 server to act as a client

➤ Internet access

Estimated completion time: **30–45 minutes**

ACTIVITY

The servers used in this activity will be referred to as Server-X and Server-Y. Please substitute the names of your servers for these names.

1. Log on to Server-X as Administrator.

2. Click **Start**, **Programs**, **Administrative Tools**, **Routing and Remote Access**.

3. Expand **IP Routing** and click **General**.

4. Right-click the **Internal** NIC and select **Properties**.

5. Click the **Input Filters** button.

6. Click **Add**.

7. Enter the information shown in Figure 11-12.

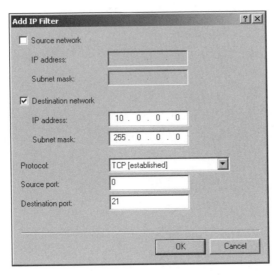

| Add IP Filter | ? X |

☐ Source network

IP address: [　　　　　]

Subnet mask: [　　　　　]

☑ Destination network

IP address: [10 . 0 . 0 . 0]

Subnet mask: [255 . 0 . 0 . 0]

Protocol: [TCP [established] ▼]

Source port: [0]

Destination port: [21]

[OK] [Cancel]

Figure 11-12   Creating an ftp output filter

8. Click **OK**.

9. Select the **Receive all packets except those that meet the criteria below** radio button.

10. Click **OK**.

11. Click **OK**.

12. Log on to Server-Y as Administrator.

13. Click **Start**, **Run**, and type **cmd**.

14. At the command line, type **ftp server-x**.

15. You will be notified that you are connected to Server-x, but the connection will time out, and you will receive the message: "Connection closed by remote host".

16. Type **ftp.microsoft.com** in the command line. You will connect successfully and be prompted to log on.

17. Before you proceed to other labs, you should remove both filters.

To remove the NAT input filters:

1. Click **Start**, **Programs**, **Administrative Tools**, **Routing and Remote Access**.

2. Expand **IP Routing** and click **General**.

3. Right-click the **External** NIC and select **Properties**.

11

4. Click **Output Filters** and click **Remove** for all filters.

5. Click **OK** to close the **Output Filters** window.

6. Right-click the **Internal** NIC and select **Properties**.

7. Click **Input Filters** and click **Remove** for all filters.

8. Click **OK** to close the **Input Filters** window.

9. Close all windows and log off.

Certification Objectives

Objectives for CompTIA Security+ Exam:

➤ Infrastructure Security: Security Topologies

Review Questions

1. Which of the following input filters would enable client external Web access?

    a. Source 255.255.255.255 Protocol TCP Source Port 80

    b. Source 0.0.0.0 Protocol TCP Source Port 80

    c. Source 255.255.255.255 Protocol TCP Destination Port 80

    d. Source 0.0.0.0 Protocol TCP Destination Port 80

2. Which of the following input filters would enable client ftp access? (Choose all that apply.)

    a. Source 255.255.255.255 Protocol TCP Destination Port 20

    b. Source 0.0.0.0 Protocol TCP Destination Port 20

    c. Source 255.255.255.255 Protocol TCP Destination Port 21

    d. Source 0.0.0.0 Protocol TCP Destination Port 21

3. A PPTP session should not be established directly from a NAT server because it may open potential security holes. True or False?

4. Using input and output filters replaces the need for a true firewall product. True or False?

5. Input filters should be applied to which Interface?

    a. internal

    b. external

    c. both

LAB 11.5 CONFIGURING A VLAN

Objectives

In the past, when a network connected with hubs grew and the number of collisions increased, network engineers would have to segment the network with a bridge or router. Today, most networks use switches in place of hubs because they are more efficient and can perform the same duties as a bridge. Another advantage to using a switch is the ability to create a Virtual LAN (VLAN). VLANs enable a network engineer to organize and group broadcast domains based on criteria other than physical location and can span multiple switches and sites. In this lab you will configure a switch with multiple VLANs. Note that a router is necessary to allow communications between VLANs. This works similarly to communication between multiple LANs.

After completing this lab, you will be able to:

➤ Physically connect to a Cisco 1900 series switch from a workstation

➤ Configure Hyperterminal to access the switch configuration

➤ Configure VLANs

➤ Reset the switch configuration to factory defaults

Materials Required

This lab will require the following:

➤ A Cisco 1900 switch

➤ A Windows PC with HyperTerminal installed

➤ A proprietary Cisco console port cable

➤ An RJ-45-to-DB-9 or DB-25 adapter

Estimated completion time: **15–30 minutes**

ACTIVITY

1. Shut down your PC and make sure the Cisco switch is unplugged.

2. Connect one end of the console cable to the console port on the switch.

3. Connect the other end of the cable to the COM1 or COM2 port on the PC. The RJ-45-to-DB-9 or DB-25 adapter should be connected to the PC end of the cable.

4. Click **Start**, **Programs**, **Accessories**, **Communications**, **HyperTerminal**.

5. Enter **Cisco 1900 Switch** for the Connection Description.

6. Click **OK**.

11

7. In the Connect using: box, choose **COM1** or **COM2**, depending on the port that is connected to the switch.

8. Click **OK**.

9. Enter the following settings:
   - Bits per second: **9600**
   - Data bits: **8**
   - Parity: **None**
   - Stop bits: **1**
   - Flow Control: **None**

10. Click **OK** to accept the configuration.

11. If there is no response from the switch, press **Enter**.

12. The main menu of the switch's management console should now be displayed. Press **M** to access the menu interface.

13. Type **C** to set a console password.

14. At this time, there is no password set. It is important to be very careful when setting a switch password. There is no password recovery routine as there is on a Cisco Router. Type **M** to modify the password.

15. Type **cisco** for the password, and then press **Enter**. Type **cisco** again to verify the password, and then press **Enter**.

16. Press **any key** to continue, and then type **X** to exit to the main menu.

17. Type **S** to access the system configuration menu.

18. Type **N** to name the switch, and then type **Cisco1900** and pres **Enter**.

19. Type **C**, and then enter *your name* as the contact and press **Enter**.

20. Type **L**, and enter **Classroom X** as the location, and press **Enter**. (Replace the X with your classroom number.)

21. Type **S**, and then type **1** and press **Enter** to set the switching mode to store-and-forward.

22. Type **X** to exit to the main menu.

23. Type **V** to access the VLAN menu.

24. Type **A** to add a VLAN.

25. Type **1**, and then press **Enter** to choose the Ethernet VLAN type.

26. Type **V** for VLAN name, type **Engineering**, and then press **Enter**. The name of the second VLAN is now Engineering. Note: this switch has an existing VLAN (VLAN 1) by default.

27. Type **S** to save and exit.

28. Type **A** to add a VLAN.

29. Type **1**, and then press **Enter** to choose the Ethernet VLAN type.

30. Type **N**, type **3**, and press **Enter** to create VLAN 3.

31. Type **V** for VLAN name, type **Finance**, and then press **Enter**. The name of the third VLAN is now Finance.

32. Type **S** to save and exit.

33. Type **L** to list your VLANs. Type **1, 2, 3** and press **Enter** to list VLANs 1, 2, 3.

34. If necessary, press **any key**.

35. Type **E** for VLAN membership.

36. Type **V** for VLAN assignment.

37. Type **4-8**, press **Enter**, and then type **2** to move ports 4-8 to the Engineering VLAN. Press **Enter**.

38. Type **V** for VLAN assignment.

39. Type **9-12**, press **Enter**, and then type **3** to move ports 9-12 to the Finance VLAN. Press **Enter**.

40. Type **X** to exit to the previous menu.

41. Type **X** again to exit to the main menu, and then type **X** once more to log out of the management console.

42. Type **M** to attempt to return to the switch menu interface.

43. When prompted for the password, type **cisco**.

44. Type **S** for system, and then type **F** to reset the factory defaults of the switch. Type **Y**, and then press **Enter** to confirm.

45. Close HyperTerminal. Save the switch settings when prompted.

46. Unplug the switch.

47. Remove the console cable from the switch and PC.

Certification Objectives

Objectives for CompTIA Security+ Exam:

➤ Infrastructure Security: Security Topologies: VLANs

Review Questions

1. Switching allows a network to maintain full duplex Ethernet. True or False?

2. Switches usually operate at which layer of the OSI model?

   a. Layer 1

   b. Layer 2

   c. Layer 3

   d. Layer 4

3. Which switching method reads the MAC address as soon as the packet is detected by the switch?

   a. Shared-memory

   b. Cut-through

   c. Store-and-forward

   d. Fragment-free

4. Which switching method will save the entire packet to the buffer and check it for CRC errors before sending?

   a. Shared-memory

   b. Cut-through

   c. Store-and-forward

   d. Fragment-free

5. Which switching method reads the MAC address as soon as the packet is detected but stores the first 64 bytes of the packet before sending it?

   a. Shared-memory

   b. Cut-through

   c. Store-and-forward

   d. Fragment-free

INTRUSION DETECTION

Labs included in this chapter:

➤ Lab 12.1 Installing Snort on Windows-based Systems

➤ Lab 12.2 Capturing Packets with Snort

➤ Lab 12.3 Creating a Snort Rule Set

➤ Lab 12.4 Using IDSCenter as a Front End for Snort

➤ Lab 12.5 Creating a Simple Honeypot

CompTIA Security+ Exam Objectives	
Objective	Lab
Infrastructure Security: Intrusion Detection	12.1, 12.2, 12.3, 12.4, 12.5
Infrastructure Security: Intrusion Detection: Network Based	12.2
Infrastructure Security: Intrusion Detection: Honeypots	12.5

LAB 12.1 INSTALLING SNORT ON WINDOWS-BASED SYSTEMS

Objectives

Being able to recover from a security breach is a vital part of network security. However, this is a reactive way to secure your network and may contribute to considerable downtime. A proactive approach to network security is to detect intrusions before they occur, or to have a plan for preventing them from doing damage if they do infiltrate your network. The primary proactive tool for network security is an Intrusion Detection System (IDS). An IDS functions by listening to the network for recognized attacks, then reporting the findings to a network administrator. An IDS is excellent for detecting and reporting problems, but not for repairing damage. It is still necessary for a network administrator to properly repair the damage done by a security breach. An example of an IDS is an open-source solution named Snort.

After completing this lab, you will be able to:

➤ Install WinPcap, a packet capture utility

➤ Install Snort for Windows

Materials Required

This lab will require the following:

➤ Two Windows 2000 servers

➤ Snort 1.9.x (A copy of this can be downloaded from *www.snort.org* or from the Student Download area of the Course Technology Web site at *www.course.com*.)

➤ WinPcap (A copy of this can also be downloaded from *www.snort.org* or *www.course.com*.)

➤ WinZip or similar file compression software package

Estimated completion time: **30 minutes**

ACTIVITY

The servers used in this activity will be referred to as Server-X and Server-Y. Please substitute the names of your servers for these names.

1. Log on to Server-X as Administrator.

2. Create the folder **snort** on C:\ (your local hard drive).

3. Copy **WinPcap_3_0_a3.exe** to the snort folder.

4. Double-click the **WinPcap_3_0_a3.exe** file in the snort folder.

5. Click **Next** three times. You will receive a message that WinPcap was correctly installed.

6. Click **OK**.

7. Reboot Server-X and log on as Administrator.

8. Double-click the **Snort-1.9.0-win32.exe** file to start the installation. Choose the **Custom** installation, and choose **C:\snort** as the destination folder.

9. Rename the **snort.conf** file in C:\snort to **snort.old**.

10. Open **snort.old** with Wordpad (not Notepad).

11. Save the **snort.old** file as **snort.conf** in a text format.

12. Click **Yes** to accept the format change.

13. Rename the **snort.conf.txt** file to **snort.conf**.

14. Click **Yes** to accept the change.

15. Repeat steps 1–15 above on Server-Y.

16. Log off Server-X and Server-Y.

Certification Objectives

Objectives for CompTIA Security+ Exam:

➤ Infrastructure Security: Intrusion Detection

Review Questions

1. An IDS evaluates a suspected intrusion once it has taken place and signals an alarm. True or False?

2. Which of the following IDS systems logs the information and signals an alert?

   a. network-based

   b. host-based

   c. passive

   d. reactive

3. Which of the following IDS systems responds to the suspicious activity by logging off a user or by reprogramming the firewall to block network traffic from the suspected malicious source?

   a. network-based

   b. host-based

   c. passive

   d. reactive

12

4. Which of the following IDS detection methods analyze the information they gather and compare it to large databases of attack signatures? (Choose all that apply.)

    a. anomaly

    b. misuse

    c. passive

    d. reactive

5. A firewall limits the access between networks in order to prevent intrusion and does not signal an attack from inside the network. True or False?

LAB 12.2 CAPTURING PACKETS WITH SNORT

Objectives

The first requirement of a network-based IDS is the ability to act as a sniffer on the network. Because the source of the attack is unknown, the IDS must be able to listen to anything that travels across the network. A network-based IDS looks for attack signatures that usually indicate malicious intent. Another type of IDS is host-based, which checks for signatures in log files. This type of IDS does not sniff the network, but it may examine the Windows Event logs. In this lab you will use Snort as a packet sniffer to capture ICMP packets from a ping and create log files.

After completing this lab, you will be able to:

➤ Understand how to use Snort to capture data packets

➤ View the contents of the data packets

➤ Create log files

Materials Required

This lab will require the following:

➤ Two Windows 2000 servers with Snort installed

➤ A crossover cable

Estimated completion time: **45 minutes**

ACTIVITY

The servers used in this activity will be referred to as Server-X and Server-Y. Please substitute the names of your servers for these names.

1. Unplug the network connection to the classroom network. Make sure Server-X and Server-Y are connected with a crossover cable.

2. Disable the classroom NICs.

3. Log on to Server-X as Administrator.

4. Click **Start**, **Run**, and type **cmd**.

5. Click **OK**.

6. Type **cd\snort**, and then press Enter.

7. Type **snort −v**, and then press **Enter**. You will see a screen similar to the one shown in Figure 12-1.

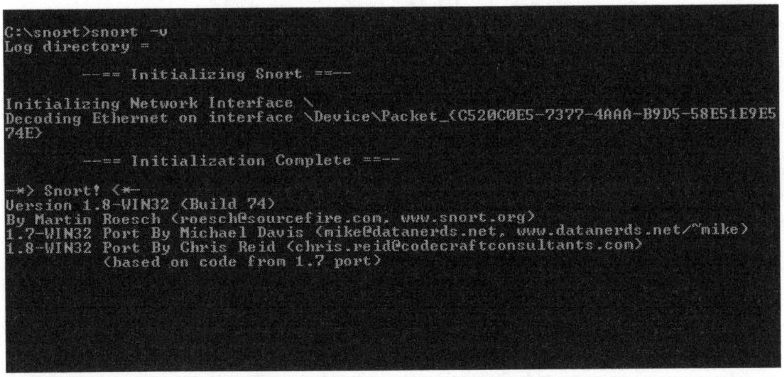

```
C:\snort>snort -v
Log directory =

        ---== Initializing Snort ==---

Initializing Network Interface \
Decoding Ethernet on interface \Device\Packet_{C520C0E5-7377-4AAA-B9D5-58E51E9E5
74E>

        ---== Initialization Complete ==---

-*> Snort! <*-
Version 1.8-WIN32 (Build 74)
By Martin Roesch (roesch@sourcefire.com, www.snort.org)
1.7-WIN32 Port By Michael Davis (mike@datanerds.net, www.datanerds.net/~mike)
1.8-WIN32 Port By Chris Reid (chris.reid@codecraftconsultants.com)
        (based on code from 1.7 port)
```

Figure 12-1   Initializing Snort

8. Log on to Server-Y as Administrator.

9. Click **Start**, **Run**, and type **cmd**.

10. Click **OK**.

11. Type **ping Server-X** and press **Enter**.

12. On Server-X, press **Ctrl+C** to view the results, as shown in Figure 12-2. Notice the **ECHO** and **ECHO REPLY**.

12

```
1.7-WIN32 Port By Michael Davis (mike@datanerds.net, www.datanerds.net/~mike)
1.8-WIN32 Port By Chris Reid (chris.reid@codecraftconsultants.com)
        (based on code from 1.7 port)
09/05-09:47:38.275050 10.10.1.1 -> 10.10.1.2
ICMP TTL:128 TOS:0x0 ID:198 IpLen:20 DgmLen:60
Type:8  Code:0  ID:2    Seq:37  ECHO
=+=+=+=+=+=+=+=+=+=+=+=+=+=+=+=+=+=+=+=+=+=+=+=+=+=+=+=+=+=+=+=+

09/05-09:47:38.275195 10.10.1.2 -> 10.10.1.1
ICMP TTL:128 TOS:0x0 ID:88 IpLen:20 DgmLen:60
Type:0  Code:0  ID:2    Seq:37  ECHO REPLY
=+=+=+=+=+=+=+=+=+=+=+=+=+=+=+=+=+=+=+=+=+=+=+=+=+=+=+=+=+=+=+=+

09/05-09:47:39.285902 10.10.1.1 -> 10.10.1.2
ICMP TTL:128 TOS:0x0 ID:199 IpLen:20 DgmLen:60
Type:8  Code:0  ID:2    Seq:38  ECHO
=+=+=+=+=+=+=+=+=+=+=+=+=+=+=+=+=+=+=+=+=+=+=+=+=+=+=+=+=+=+=+=+

09/05-09:47:39.286035 10.10.1.2 -> 10.10.1.1
ICMP TTL:128 TOS:0x0 ID:89 IpLen:20 DgmLen:60
Type:0  Code:0  ID:2    Seq:38  ECHO REPLY
=+=+=+=+=+=+=+=+=+=+=+=+=+=+=+=+=+=+=+=+=+=+=+=+=+=+=+=+=+=+=+=+

09/05-09:47:40.297322 10.10.1.1 -> 10.10.1.2
ICMP TTL:128 TOS:0x0 ID:200 IpLen:20 DgmLen:60
Type:8  Code:0  ID:2    Seq:39  ECHO
=+=+=+=+=+=+=+=+=+=+=+=+=+=+=+=+=+=+=+=+=+=+=+=+=+=+=+=+=+=+=+=+

09/05-09:47:40.297460 10.10.1.2 -> 10.10.1.1
ICMP TTL:128 TOS:0x0 ID:90 IpLen:20 DgmLen:60
Type:0  Code:0  ID:2    Seq:39  ECHO REPLY
=+=+=+=+=+=+=+=+=+=+=+=+=+=+=+=+=+=+=+=+=+=+=+=+=+=+=+=+=+=+=+=+

09/05-09:47:41.308784 10.10.1.1 -> 10.10.1.2
ICMP TTL:128 TOS:0x0 ID:201 IpLen:20 DgmLen:60
Type:8  Code:0  ID:2    Seq:40  ECHO
=+=+=+=+=+=+=+=+=+=+=+=+=+=+=+=+=+=+=+=+=+=+=+=+=+=+=+=+=+=+=+=+

09/05-09:47:41.308922 10.10.1.2 -> 10.10.1.1
ICMP TTL:128 TOS:0x0 ID:91 IpLen:20 DgmLen:60
Type:0  Code:0  ID:2    Seq:40  ECHO REPLY
=+=+=+=+=+=+=+=+=+=+=+=+=+=+=+=+=+=+=+=+=+=+=+=+=+=+=+=+=+=+=+=+
```

Figure 12-2   A Snort ping capture

13. Scroll down the command windows to view the statistics, as shown in Figure 12-3. Notice that the protocol used was ICMP.

```
Snort analyzed 8 out of 8 packets, dropping 0(0.000%) packets

Breakdown by protocol:                    Action Stats:
    TCP: 0          (0.000%)              ALERTS: 0
    UDP: 0          (0.000%)              LOGGED: 0
   ICMP: 8          (100.000%)            PASSED: 0
    ARP: 0          (0.000%)
   IPv6: 0          (0.000%)
    IPX: 0          (0.000%)
  OTHER: 0          (0.000%)
DISCARD: 0          (0.000%)
=================================================================
Fragmentation Stats:
Fragmented IP Packets: 0            (0.000%)
     Fragment Trackers: 0
    Rebuilt IP Packets: 0
    Frag elements used: 0
Discarded(incomplete): 0
   Discarded(timeout): 0
  Frag2 memory faults: 0
=================================================================
TCP Stream Reassembly Stats:
     TCP Packets Used: 0            (0.000%)
      Stream Trackers: 0
       Stream flushes: 0
        Segments used: 0
 Stream4 Memory Faults: 0
=================================================================
pcap_loop: read error: PacketReceivePacket failedpcap_stats: PacketGetStats erro
r
Snort received signal 3, exiting

C:\snort>
```

Figure 12-3   Snort ping capture statistics

14. On Server-X, type **snort –v –d** at the command line to view the packet data.

15. Press **Enter**.

16. On Server-Y, type **ping Server-X** and press **Enter**.

17. On Server-X, press **Ctrl+C** to view the results. You will see a screen similar to the one shown in Figure 12-4.

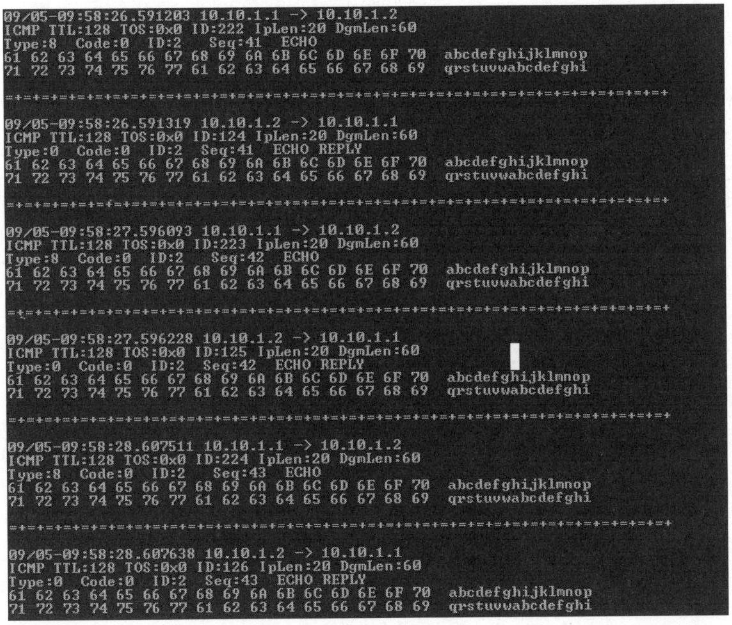

```
09/05-09:58:26.591203 10.10.1.1 -> 10.10.1.2
ICMP TTL:128 TOS:0x0 ID:222 IpLen:20 DgmLen:60
Type:8  Code:0  ID:2    Seq:41   ECHO
61 62 63 64 65 66 67 68 69 6A 6B 6C 6D 6E 6F 70   abcdefghijklmnop
71 72 73 74 75 76 77 61 62 63 64 65 66 67 68 69   qrstuvwabcdefghi

=+=+=+=+=+=+=+=+=+=+=+=+=+=+=+=+=+=+=+=+=+=+=+=+=+=+=+=+=+=+=+=+

09/05-09:58:26.591319 10.10.1.2 -> 10.10.1.1
ICMP TTL:128 TOS:0x0 ID:124 IpLen:20 DgmLen:60
Type:0  Code:0  ID:2    Seq:41   ECHO REPLY
61 62 63 64 65 66 67 68 69 6A 6B 6C 6D 6E 6F 70   abcdefghijklmnop
71 72 73 74 75 76 77 61 62 63 64 65 66 67 68 69   qrstuvwabcdefghi

=+=+=+=+=+=+=+=+=+=+=+=+=+=+=+=+=+=+=+=+=+=+=+=+=+=+=+=+=+=+=+=+

09/05-09:58:27.596093 10.10.1.1 -> 10.10.1.2
ICMP TTL:128 TOS:0x0 ID:223 IpLen:20 DgmLen:60
Type:8  Code:0  ID:2    Seq:42   ECHO
61 62 63 64 65 66 67 68 69 6A 6B 6C 6D 6E 6F 70   abcdefghijklmnop
71 72 73 74 75 76 77 61 62 63 64 65 66 67 68 69   qrstuvwabcdefghi

=+=+=+=+=+=+=+=+=+=+=+=+=+=+=+=+=+=+=+=+=+=+=+=+=+=+=+=+=+=+=+=+

09/05-09:58:27.596228 10.10.1.2 -> 10.10.1.1
ICMP TTL:128 TOS:0x0 ID:125 IpLen:20 DgmLen:60
Type:0  Code:0  ID:2    Seq:42   ECHO REPLY
61 62 63 64 65 66 67 68 69 6A 6B 6C 6D 6E 6F 70   abcdefghijklmnop
71 72 73 74 75 76 77 61 62 63 64 65 66 67 68 69   qrstuvwabcdefghi

=+=+=+=+=+=+=+=+=+=+=+=+=+=+=+=+=+=+=+=+=+=+=+=+=+=+=+=+=+=+=+=+

09/05-09:58:28.607511 10.10.1.1 -> 10.10.1.2
ICMP TTL:128 TOS:0x0 ID:224 IpLen:20 DgmLen:60
Type:8  Code:0  ID:2    Seq:43   ECHO
61 62 63 64 65 66 67 68 69 6A 6B 6C 6D 6E 6F 70   abcdefghijklmnop
71 72 73 74 75 76 77 61 62 63 64 65 66 67 68 69   qrstuvwabcdefghi

=+=+=+=+=+=+=+=+=+=+=+=+=+=+=+=+=+=+=+=+=+=+=+=+=+=+=+=+=+=+=+=+

09/05-09:58:28.607638 10.10.1.2 -> 10.10.1.1
ICMP TTL:128 TOS:0x0 ID:126 IpLen:20 DgmLen:60
Type:0  Code:0  ID:2    Seq:43   ECHO REPLY
61 62 63 64 65 66 67 68 69 6A 6B 6C 6D 6E 6F 70   abcdefghijklmnop
71 72 73 74 75 76 77 61 62 63 64 65 66 67 68 69   qrstuvwabcdefghi
```

Figure 12-4   A Snort ping capture with data

18. On Server-X, create a folder named **log** in C:\snort.

19. Type **snort –dev –l \snort\log** at the command line and press **Enter**.

20. Ping Server-X from Server-Y.

21. On Server-X, press **Ctrl+C**.

22. Navigate to the C:\snort\log folder and examine the contents. Use Notepad to open the files.

23. Repeat steps 1-22 above on Server-Y.

24. Close all Windows and log off Server-X and Server-Y.

Certification Objectives

Objectives for CompTIA Security+ Exam:

➤ Infrastructure Security: Intrusion Detection: Network-based

Review Questions

1. Which IDS method is operating system–dependent?
   a. host-based
   b. log-based
   c. network-based
   d. event-based

2. Which of the following is a technique for recognizing an attack signature?
   a. frequency
   b. pattern
   c. correlation
   d. statistical
   e. all of the above

3. Which method of IDS is best suited for detecting Trojan horses such as BackOrifice?
   a. host-based
   b. log-based
   c. network-based
   d. event-based

4. Which method of IDS is capable of real-time detection?
   a. host-based
   b. log-based
   c. network-based
   d. event-based

5. Which method of IDS is best suited for encrypted and switched environments?
   a. host-based
   b. log-based
   c. network-based
   d. event-based

LAB 12.3 CREATING A SNORT RULE SET

Objectives

While an IDS can be very useful in detecting intrusions, it can also produce more information than necessary in the log files. If the log files are too large to manage, they are not useful. An IDS can sniff all traffic, but the ability to create rules allows a network engineer to filter just the necessary signatures. For example, if you are monitoring a network that contains a Web server, it wouldn't make sense to log requests on port 80. But you may want to log any Telnet and other protocols for attempts on that network to see if someone is trying to exploit a weakness. In this lab you will create a simple Snort rule to alert you when the ICMP protocol is used.

After completing this lab, you will be able to:

➤ Create a Snort rule set

➤ Test the rules set on the network

Materials Required

This lab will require the following:

➤ Two Windows 2000 servers with Snort and all of the latest service packs and hotfixes installed

Estimated completion time: **15–20 minutes**

ACTIVITY

The servers used in this activity will be referred to as Server-X and Server-Y. Please substitute the names of your servers for these names.

1. Log on to Server-X as Administrator.

2. Click **Start**, **Run**, and type **notepad**.

3. Click **OK**.

4. Enter the information shown in Figure 12-5.

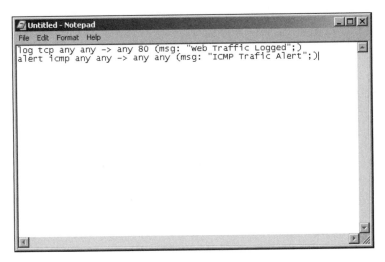

Figure 12-5   A Snort rule set

5. Save the file as **c:\snort\new.rules**. Close Notepad.

6. On Server-X, click **Start**, **Run**, and then type **cmd**. Click **OK**.

7. Type **cd\snort** in the command line, then press **Enter**.

8. Type **snort –c \snort\new.rules –l \snort\log** at the command line, then press **Enter**.

9. From Server-Y, open Internet Explorer and enter **Server-X** in the address box. Press **Enter**.

10. On Server-X, press **Ctrl+C**.

11. Navigate to the **C:\snort\log** folder.

12. Examine the **Web Traffic Logged in the TCP_*-80.ids** file. It should look similar to the file shown in Figure 12-6.

Figure 12-6   A Snort log file containing Web traffic

13. On Server-X, type **snort –c \snort\new.rules –l \snort\log**, then press **Enter**.

14. On Server-Y, ping Server-X.

15. On Server-X, press **Ctrl+C**.

16. Navigate to the **C:\snort\log** folder.

17. Examine the contents of the **alert.ids** file. It should look similar to the file shown in Figure 12-7.

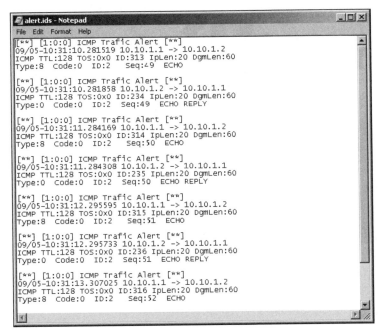

Figure 12-7   A Snort ICMP traffic alert log

18. Repeat steps 1–17 above on Server-Y.

19. Close all Windows and log off Server-X and Server-Y.

12

Certification Objectives

Objectives for CompTIA Security+ Exam:

➤ Infrastructure Security: Intrusion Detection

Review Questions

1. Which of the following is equivalent to all IP addresses when creating Snort rules?

   a. all

   b. any

   c. 0.0.0.0

   d. 255.255.255.255

2. Which of the following will log tcp traffic from any port going to ports less than or equal to 6000 on the 192.168.1.0 network?

   a. log tcp any any -> 192.168.1.0/24 :6000

   b. log tcp any any -> 192.168.1.0/24 <=6000

   c. log udp any any -> 192.168.1.0/24 :6000

   d. log tcp any any -> 192.168.1.0/24 any

3. Which of the following protocols can Snort analyze?

a. Tcp

b. Udp

c. Icmp

d. Ip

e. all of the above

4. Which of the following operators is used to log port ranges?

a. >

b. <

c. :

d. ;

5. Which of the following Snort keywords will print a message in alerts and packet logs?

a. print

b. msg

c. type

d. alert

LAB 12.4 USING IDSCENTER AS A FRONT END FOR SNORT

Objectives

An IDS can be very helpful in protecting a network from intrusions, but the programs themselves are usually not easy to use. You may have noticed in the previous labs that Snort is a very powerful tool, but it is difficult to work with. This is not uncommon in the security field, but something that has been addressed. One way to fix this problem is to use a front-end program that does the difficult work. In this lab you will use IDScenter to make Snort easier to use and also offer some additional features not available with the command line application.

After completing this lab, you will be able to:

➤ Configure Windows services and processes

➤ Disable unnecessary services

Materials Required:

This lab will require the following:

➤ Two Windows 2000 servers with Snort installed

➤ IDScenter (This program can be downloaded from the Packx Web site at *www.packx.net*, or from the Student Download area of the Course Technology Web site at *www.course.com*.)

Estimated completion time: **45 minutes**

ACTIVITY

The servers used in this activity will be referred to as Server-X and Server-Y. Please substitute the names of your servers for these names.

1. Log on to Server-X as Administrator.

2. Run the **setup.exe** file from the idscenter.zip file.

3. The Installation wizard will begin. Click **Next**.

4. Click **Next** to accept the default installation location **C:\Program Files\IDScenter**.

5. Click **Next** to select the Program Group **Snort IDScenter**.

6. Click **Install**.

7. Uncheck the **View info.txt** check box.

8. Click **Finish**.

9. Double-click the **IDScenter** icon on the desktop. The program will load and put an icon in the system tray.

10. Double-click the icon in the system tray.

11. In the Snort setup section, choose the location of the snort.exe file, as shown in Figure 12-8.

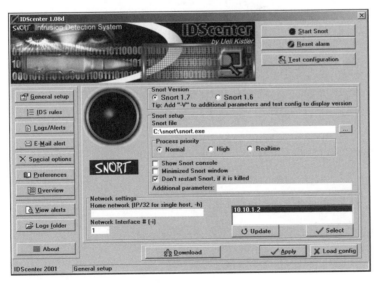

Figure 12-8   IDScenter opening screen

12. Enter *<server-X IP address>*/32 in the Home Network Section, as shown in Figure 12-9.

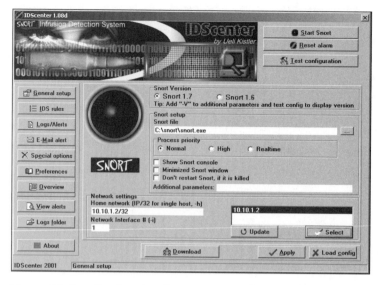

Figure 12-9 Configuring Snort setup and network settings

13. Click the **IDS rules** button.

14. Choose the **new.rules** file you created in the previous lab exercise for the Snort IDS ruleset, as shown in Figure 12-10.

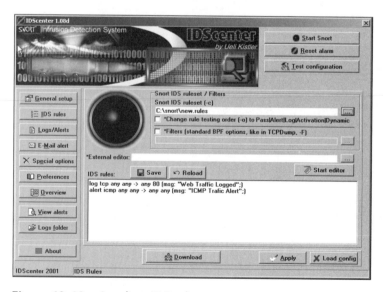

Figure 12-10 Loading IDS rules

15. Click the **Logs/Alerts** button.

16. Enter **C:\snort\log** in the Set directory for Snort logfiles.

17. Check the **Set alert mode (–A)** box.

18. Check the **Dump the raw packets (–X)** box, as shown in Figure 12-11.

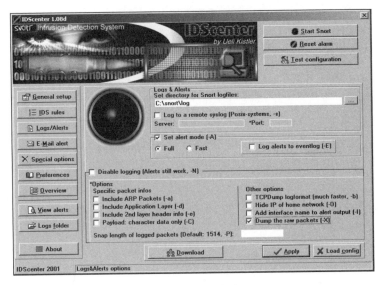

Figure 12-11   Configuring logs and alerts

19. Click the **Special options** button.

20. Check the ***Start this program when receiving an alert** box.

21. Enter **net send 10.10.1.2 Alert, Check the Snort logs!**, as shown in Figure 12-12. *Note: replace 10.10.1.2 with your IP address.*

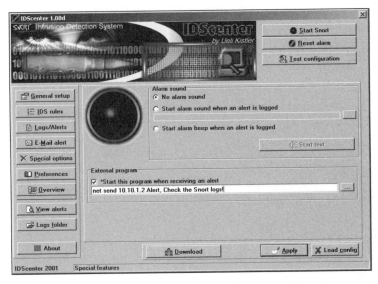

Figure 12-12   Run an external program to send an administrative alert

22. Click the **Overview** button, and then click **Apply**. Notice the Snort command line, shown in Figure 12-13.

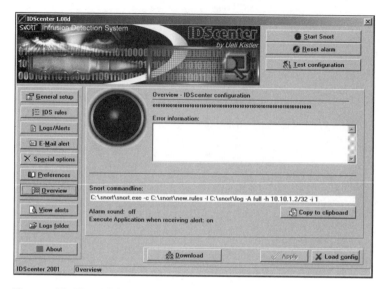

Figure 12-13   IDScenter Snort configuration overview

23. Click **Start Snort**.

24. Ping Server-X from Server-Y. You will receive a message similar to the one shown in Figure 12-14.

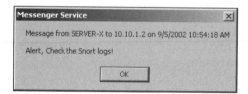

Figure 12-14   An IDScenter alert message

25. Click **OK** to close the message.

26. Click the **View alerts** button to view the details.

27. Click **Stop Snort**.

28. Repeat steps 1–27 above on Server-Y.

29. Close all Windows and log off Server-X and Server-Y.

Certification Objectives

Objectives for CompTIA Security+ Exam:

➤ Infrastructure Security: Intrusion Detection

Review Questions

1. IDScenter can alert an administrator with which of the following?

    a. e-mail

    b. sound

    c. visual alerts

    d. all of the above

2. The Snort command line application offers a testing feature that is not available in IDScenter. True or False?

3. IDScenter can create log files in which of the following formats? (Choose all that apply.)

    a. text

    b. HTML

    c. PDF

    d. XML

    e. all of the above

4. IDScenter can execute a program when an attack is detected. True or False?

5. If you want to be informed about all attacks coming from a WAN, you should deploy the IDS:

    a. in front of a firewall

    b. behind a firewall

    c. on a firewall

    d. in place of a firewall

12

LAB 12.5 CREATING A SIMPLE HONEYPOT

Objectives

Honeypots are systems that are designed to be probed, attacked, and even compromised to help reduce risk in an organization. There are two types of honeypots: production, which is used to protect a network by acting as a decoy system, and research, which is used to gain information on the hacker community and to test the strength of your network security. While honeypots may not be good for prevention, they can be an excellent point of detection. Because of their simple design, they are also easy to configure. In this lab you will install, configure, and test a simple honeypot program, BackOfficer.

After completing this lab, you will be able to:

➤ Install and configure BackOfficer

➤ Detect a Telnet attempt

Materials Required

This lab will require the following:

➤ Two Windows 2000 servers with all of the latest service packs and hotfixes installed

➤ BackOfficer (This can be downloaded from *www.nfr.com/products/bof/* or from the Student Downloads area of the Course Technology Web site at *www.course.com.*)

Estimated completion time: **20–25 minutes**

ACTIVITY

The servers used in this activity will be referred to as Server-X and Server-Y. Please substitute the names of your servers for these names.

1. Log on to Server-X as Administrator.

2. Double-click the **nfrbofl.exe** file.

3. Click **OK** to accept the default installation location **C:\Program Files\ NFR\BackOfficer Friendly**.

4. You will receive the message shown in Figure 12-15.

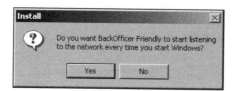

Figure 12-15   BackOfficer option to start concurrently with Windows

5. Click **Yes**. You will receive a second message, shown in Figure 12-16.

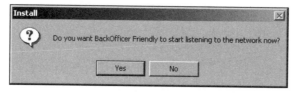

Figure 12-16   Option to start BackOfficer now

6. Click **Yes**.

7. Click **OK** to finish. Notice the new icon in the system tray.

8. Right-click the **BackOfficer** icon in the system tray, and then click **Details**.

9. Click **Options**.

10. Select **Listen for Telnet**.

11. On Server-Y, type **telnet server-x**. Notice the telnet detection on Server-X, as shown in Figure 12-17.

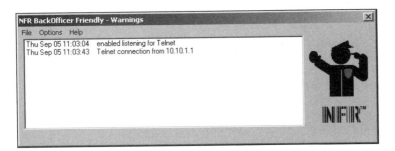

Figure 12-17   BackOfficer Telnet detection

12. Click **Options** and select **Listen for HTTP**.

13. You will receive the message shown in Figure 12-18.

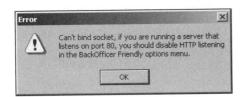

Figure 12-18   BackOfficer error message

 The purpose of the Honeypot is to keep an eye on potential attacks as well as providing a potential hacker with a fake target. If you want to listen for HTTP, disable the IIS service.

14. Repeat steps 1–13 above on Server-Y.

15. Close all Windows and log off Server-X and Server-Y.

Certification Objectives

Objectives for CompTIA Security+ Exam:

➤ Infrastructure Security: Intrusion Detection: Honeypots

Review Questions

1. A honeypot contains no data or applications critical to the company but has enough interesting data to lure a hacker. True or False?

2. Honeypots are most successful on which of the following servers? (Choose all that apply.)

   a. File

   b. Print

   c. Web

   d. DNS

3. Which of the following is another term used to describe a honeypot?

   a. sacrificial lamb

   b. decoy

   c. booby trap

   d. all of the above

4. Which of the following is a function that a honeypot can provide? (Choose all that apply.)

   a. prevention

   b. detection

   c. reaction

   d. correction

   e. all of the above

5. The most commonly used honeypot is a research honeypot. True or False?

CHAPTER THIRTEEN

SECURITY BASELINES

Labs included in this chapter:

➤ Lab 13.1 Defining Security Templates in Windows 2000

➤ Lab 13.2 Managing Windows 2000 Security Templates

➤ Lab 13.3 Using the IIS Lockdown Wizard

➤ Lab 13.4 Resetting the Changes Made by IISLockdown and Security Templates

➤ Lab 13.5 Using the Microsoft Baseline Security Analyzer

CompTIA Security+ Exam Objectives	
Objective	**Lab**
Infrastructure Security: Security Baselines	13.1, 13.2, 13.3, 13.4, 13.5

LAB 13.1 DEFINING SECURITY TEMPLATES IN WINDOWS 2000

Objectives

One of the more difficult tasks for an administrator is determining the appropriate security settings for a network. There are so many possibilities that it is very easy to miss an important setting, often resulting in a network full of security holes. Microsoft has created security templates to assist administrators with this task. In addition to providing predefined templates, Microsoft also provides administrators with the ability to create custom templates. In this lab you will create a custom security template and manually adjust the security settings.

After completing this lab, you will be able to:

> ➤ Import Windows 2000 security templates

> ➤ Configure security settings for a custom template

Materials Required

This lab will require the following:

> ➤ A Windows 2000 server

> ➤ Administrator access to the server

Estimated completion time: **30–45 minutes**

ACTIVITY

1. Log on to your server as Administrator.

2. Click **Start**, **Run**, type **mmc,** and then press **Enter**.

3. Click **Console, Add/Remove Snap-in**.

4. Click **Add**.

5. Select **Security Templates**, as shown in Figure 13-1.

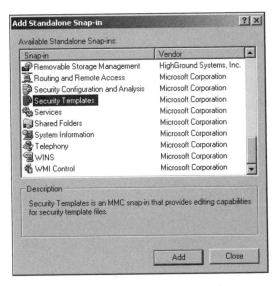

Figure 13-1   Security Templates Snap-in

6. Click **Add**, and then click **Close**.

7. Click **OK**.

8. Expand **Security Templates**.

9. Expand **C:\Winnt\Security\Templates**, as shown in Figure 13-2.

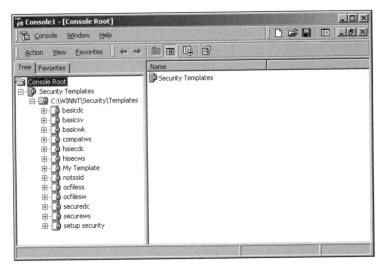

Figure 13-2   Security Templates expanded

10. Right-click **C:\Winnt\Security\Templates** and select **New template**.

11. Enter **My Template** for the template name and leave the description blank.

12. Click **OK**.

13. Expand **My Template**, as shown in Figure 13-3.

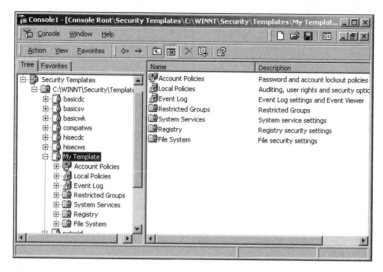

Figure 13-3 A new template named My Template

14. Right-click **Restricted Groups**.

15. Click **Add group**.

16. Click **Browse**.

17. Select **Administrators** and then click **Add**.

18. Click **OK**.

19. Click **OK**.

20. Right-click **Registry**.

21. Select **Add Key**.

22. Select **MACHINE**.

23. Click **OK**.

24. Remove the **Everyone Group** and add **Administrators**.

25. Check the box to grant Administrators **Full Control**, as shown in Figure 13-4.

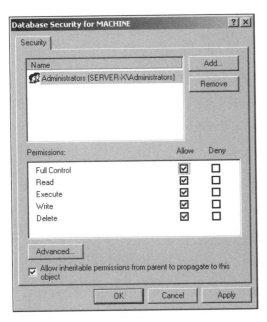

Figure 13-4   Adjusted security with only Administrators having access

26. Add **Users** and keep the default Read and Execute permissions.

27. Click **OK**.

28. Click **OK** to Configure this key then...Propagate inheritable permissions to all subkeys, as shown in Figure 13-5.

13

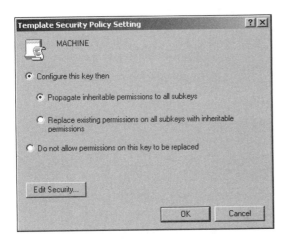

Figure 13-5   Template Security Policy Setting warning message

29. Close the Console1 Window.

30. Save the Console with the name **My Console**.

31. Click **Yes** to save the Security Template.

32. Log off Administrator.

Certification Objectives

Objectives for CompTIA Security+ Exam:

➤ Infrastructure Security: Security Baselines

Review Questions

1. Which MMC snap-in is used to provide a centralized method of defining security?

   a. Computer Management

   b. Security Configuration and Analysis

   c. Security Templates

   d. Services

2. Security Templates can be used to create new security parameters. True or False?

3. Which of the following is used to set security for user rights and logging for security events in a security template?

   a. Account policies

   b. Local policies

   c. Restricted groups

   d. Registry

4. Which of the following is used to set security for local registry keys? (Choose all that apply.)

   a. regedit

   b. Local policies section of a security template

   c. Registry section of a security template

   d. regedt32

5. The Local Group Policy is used to apply security templates, but these policies cannot be used to override a domain-based policy. True or False?

LAB 13.2 MANAGING WINDOWS 2000 SECURITY TEMPLATES

Objectives

There may be an occasion when an administrator does not have the time or knowledge to secure a server manually with a custom template. As mentioned in the previous lab, Microsoft has created predefined security templates. These templates have three primary levels: basic, secure, and high secure. The issues surrounding the use of these templates are unknown. Since the administrator is relying on Microsoft to secure the server, the settings are difficult to track. In this lab you will apply a security template and evaluate the results.

After completing this lab, you will be able to:

➤ Apply a Windows 2000 security template

➤ Restore the default security settings

Materials Required

This lab will require the following:

➤ A Windows 2000 server

➤ Administrator access to the server

Estimated completion time: **20–25 minutes**

ACTIVITY

1. Log on to your server as Administrator.

2. Click **Start**, **Programs**, **Administrative Tools** and select **My Console**.

3. Click **Console**, **Add/Remove Snap-in**.

4. Click **Add**.

5. Select **Security Configuration and Analysis**.

6. Click **Add**, and then click **Close**.

7. Click **OK**.

8. Right-click **Security Configuration and Analysis**.

9. Click **Open database**.

10. Enter **My Database.sdb** for the name, and then click **Open**.

11. Select the **securedc.inf** template to import.

12. Click **Open**.

13. Right-click **Security Configuration and Analysis**.

14. Select **Configure Computer Now**.

15. Click **OK** to use My Database.log, as shown in Figure 13-6.

13

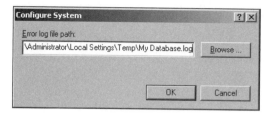

Figure 13-6   Database location

16. Right-click **Security Configuration and Analysis**.

17. Select **Analyze Computer Now…**.

18. Click **OK** to use the My Database.log file.

19. Right-click **Security Configuration and Analysis**.

20. Select **View Log File** from the shortcut menu. You will see a screen similar to the one shown in Figure 13-7.

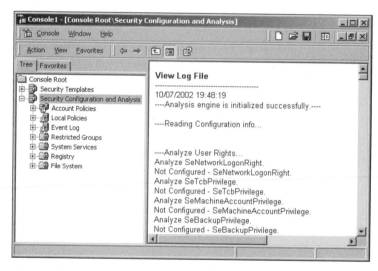

Figure 13-7   Sample configuration log file (partial)

21. Explore the log file to see the changes made.

22. Close all windows and log off Administrator.

Certification Objectives

Objectives for CompTIA Security+ Exam:

> ➤ Infrastructure Security: Security Baselines

Review Questions

1. Which of the following security templates can be used on a workstation? (Choose all that apply.)

   a. compatws

   b. hisecdc

   c. hisecws

   d. securews

2. Which of the following security templates is more likely to cause a problem with access to the server?

   a. bascicdc

   b. highsecdc

   c. securedc

   d. the absence of a security template

3. The password policy set by the hisecdc template is identical to the securedc template. True or False?

4. Programs on a workstation that was upgraded from Windows NT 4 to Windows 2000 fail to run as a member of the local user group. Which of the following security templates can be used?

   a. basicws

   b. compatsw

   c. compatws

   d. basicsw

5. What number of characters is the minimum password length requirement once the hisecdc is applied?

   a. 0

   b. 7

   c. 8

   d. 14

13

LAB 13.3 USING THE IIS LOCKDOWN WIZARD

Objectives

Microsoft has long had a reputation for releasing feature-rich products that are full of security holes. More recently, Microsoft has decided to take a "security first" approach. Internet Information Server (IIS) is well-known for having security flaws. However, some of these flaws are due to poor administration and have nothing to do with the actual code. IIS Lockdown is a wizard that was created to assist administrators in making an IIS server more secure. In this lab you will run the IISLockdown Wizard and evaluate the changes made.

After completing this lab, you will be able to:

➤ Run the IISLockdown wizard to secure an IIS server

➤ Run IISLockdown to reset the default configuration

Materials Required

This lab will require the following:

➤ A Windows 2000 server

➤ IIS Lockdown Wizard (This file, named iislockd.exe, can be downloaded from *www.microsoft.com/Downloads*.)

➤ Administrator access to the server

Estimated completion time: **20–25 minutes**

ACTIVITY

1. Log on to your server as Administrator.

2. Double-click **iislockd.exe**.

3. Click **Next** on the Welcome Page.

4. Click **I agree** on the License Agreement page.

5. Click **Next**.

6. Select the **Static Web server** template, as shown in Figure 13-8.

7. Click **View Template Settings**.

8. Click **Next**.

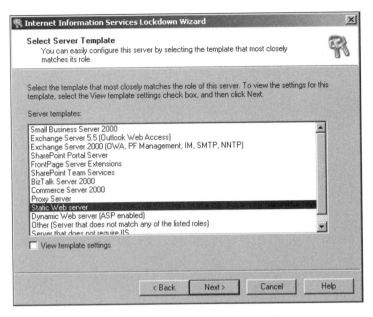

Figure 13-8   Static Web server security template

9. Select the **File Transfer Protocol (FTP)** box, as shown in Figure 13-9. Note: Web Service is checked by default. If necessary, uncheck any other options.

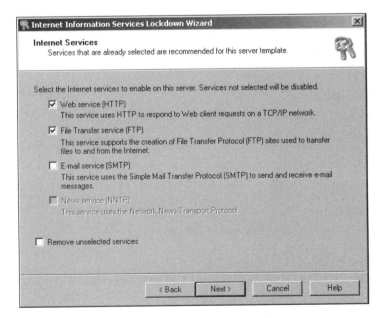

Figure 13-9   Enable or disable Internet services

10. Click **Next**.

11. Click **Next** to disable all script maps, as shown in Figure 13-10.

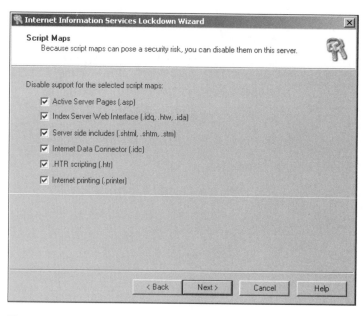

Figure 13-10   Script maps to disable

12. Click **Next** to accept the additional security defaults, as shown in Figure 13-11.

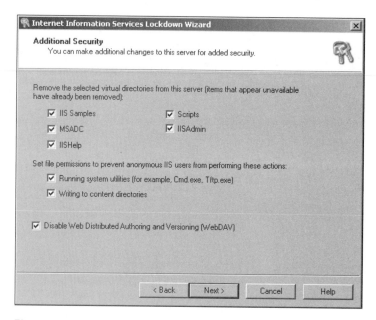

Figure 13-11   Additional security options

13. Uncheck the **Install URLScan** box, and then click **Next**.

14. Click **Next** to apply the settings.

15. Click **Yes** if you are prompted with the digital signature message shown in Figure 13–12.

Figure 13-12   Digital signature not found message

16. Once the process is finished click **View Report** to see what happened.

17. Close the report then click **Next**.

18. Click **Finish**.

19. Close all windows and log off Administrator.

Certification Objectives

Objectives for CompTIA Security+ Exam:

➤ Infrastructure Security: Security Baselines

Review Questions

1. Systems that are deployed using nonstandard processes and are at odds with the company policies are known as _____ systems.

   a. test

   b. invalid

   c. rogue

   d. insecure

2. The IISLockdown Tool can be used to secure which of the following versions of IIS? (Choose all that apply.)

   a. 2.0

   b. 3.0

   c. 4.0

   d. 5.0

3. Which of the following tools can be used to ensure that a Web server will only respond to valid requests?

   a. IISLockdown

   b. URLScan

   c. URLSecurity

   d. IISUrl

4. IISLockdown can also be used to remove or disable which of the following services?

   a. HTTP

   b. FTP

   c. SMTP

   d. NNTP

   e. all of the above

5. The IISLockdown Wizard works by turning off unnecessary features to reduce the attack possibilities of an attacker. True or False?

LAB 13.4 RESETTING THE CHANGES MADE BY IISLOCKDOWN AND SECURITY TEMPLATES

Objectives

There may be times when an administrator applies security settings that cause unexpected results on a server. These results may cause downtime and aggravation for both users and administrators. Microsoft has created a method to restore the default settings of a server in the event that a security template causes problems with the server. IISLockdown can also cause unexpected results that may require the settings to be returned to the default values. In this lab you restore the settings changed by IISLockdown and a security template.

After completing this lab, you will be able to:

➤ Undo changes made by IISLockdown

➤ Reset the default settings changed by a security template

Materials Required

This lab will require the following:

➤ A Windows 2000 server with all of the latest service packs and hotfixes installed

Estimated completion time: **15–20 minutes**

ACTIVITY

1. Log on to your server as Administrator.

2. Double-click **iislockd.exe**.

3. Click **Next**. You will receive the message shown in Figure 13-13.

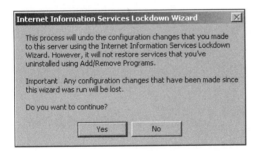

Internet Information Services Lockdown Wizard

This process will undo the configuration changes that you made to this server using the Internet Information Services Lockdown Wizard. However, it will not restore services that you've uninstalled using Add/Remove Programs.

Important   Any configuration changes that have been made since this wizard was run will be lost.

Do you want to continue?

[Yes]   [No]

Figure 13-13   IISLockdown removal warning message

13

4. Click **Yes** to undo changes.

5. Once the wizard is complete, click **Next**, and then click **Finish**.

6. To reset the default security settings, click **Start**, **Run**, and then type **cmd**. Press **Enter**.

7. Type: **secedit /configure /cfg %windir%\repair\secsetup.inf /db secsetup.sbd /verbose** and press Enter. You will see a screen similar to the one shown in Figure 13-14.

Figure 13-14   Secedit command syntax and results

8. Notice the message about missing files. This is OK, but open the **%windir\security\logs\scesrv.log** file with Notepad to see what actually changed.

9. Close all windows and log off Administrator.

Certification Objectives

Objectives for CompTIA Security+ Exam:

➤ Infrastructure Security: Security Baselines

Review Questions

1. Which of the following tools should be used prior to running IISLockdown?

    a. secedit

    b. chkntfs

    c. HFNetChk

    d. secfix

2. If the IISLockdown wizard causes problems with Exchange or Microsoft Outlook Web Access a user can run the IISLockdown wizard again to undo the changes. True or False?

3. You have applied a local security policy using a predefined security template, but the settings do not work. Which of the following is the most likely problem?

    a. You cannot apply local security policies

    b. There is a domain security policy

    c. The computer is not a member of a domain

    d. The computer is a member of a workgroup

4. Which of the following tools can be used to reset the changes made by a security template?

   a. secedit

   b. chkntfs

   c. HFNetChk

   d. secfix

5. Which of the following templates, if applied to a workstation, would require you to undo the changes?

   a. hisecws

   b. securews

   c. compatws

   d. hisecdc

LAB 13.5 USING THE MICROSOFT BASELINE SECURITY ANALYZER

Objectives

One complaint that administrators have had with securing Microsoft products is the lack of a tool that checks the entire system for security configuration flaws. Microsoft responded to this complaint with their Baseline Security Analyzer (MBSA). MBSA can scan local and remote machines for security issues with Windows NT 4, Windows 2000, Windows XP, IIS, SQL Server, Internet Explorer, and Office. Reports are generated with details after the scan is complete. In this lab you will install MBSA and view the results.

After completing this lab, you will be able to:

➤ Install MBSA

➤ View an MBSA report to determine what fixes are necessary

Materials Required

This lab will require the following:

➤ A Windows 2000 server

➤ Mbsasetup.msi (This file can be downloaded from *http://download.microsoft.com/download/win2000platform/Install/1.0/NT5XP/EN-US/mbsasetup.msi.*)

➤ Administrator access to the server

13

Estimated completion time: **20–25 minutes**

ACTIVITY

1. Log on to your server as Administrator.

2. Double-click the **mbsasetup.msi** file.

3. Click **Next** to start the wizard.

4. Click **I accept the license agreement**.

5. Click **Next** to accept the default User Information.

6. Click **Next** to use the default folder.

7. Click **Next** to accept the default install options.

8. Click **Next** to accept the default Select Features.

9. Click **Next** to install the application. The window shown in Figure 13-15 will pop up.

Figure 13-15   Microsoft Baseline Security Analyzer Wizard opening screen

10. Click **Scan a computer**.

11. Click **Start scan**, as shown in Figure 13-16.

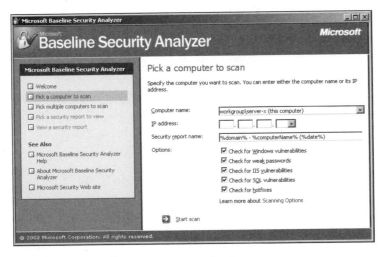

Figure 13-16   Choosing a computer to scan

12. Click **Yes** when the security warning shown in Figure 13–17 appears.

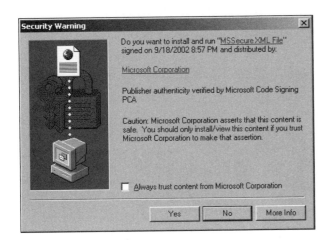

Figure 13-17   Security warning to allow Microsoft to install a program to run MBSA

13. Once the scan is complete view the report. Notice that the report shows what was scanned, the results of the scan, and how to fix any problems.

14. Close the **Report** window.

15. Click **Finish**.

16. Close all windows and log off Administrator.

Certification Objectives

Objectives for CompTIA Security+ Exam:

➤ Infrastructure Security: Security Baselines

Review Questions

1. Which of the following is a command line tool that can be used to check the patch status of all machines on a network?

   a. secedt

   b. HFNetChk

   c. chkntfs

   d. PatchChk

2. Which of the following is a graphical tool that can be used to check the patch status of all machines on a network?

   a. MBNA

   b. MBSA

   c. MBSC

   d. MCSE

3. On which of the following operating systems can the Microsoft Baseline Security Analyzer be installed? (Choose all that apply.)

   a. Windows 2000

   b. Windows NT

   c. Windows XP

   d. Windows 9.x

4. On which of the following operating systems can the Microsoft Baseline Security Analyzer scan for missing patches? (Choose all that apply.)

   a. Windows 2000

   b. Windows NT

   c. Windows XP

   d. Windows 9.x

5. On which of the following applications can the Microsoft Baseline Security Analyzer scan for missing patches? (Choose all that apply.)

   a. Internet Information Services

   b. SQL Server

   c. Windows Explorer

   d. Internet Explorer

CHAPTER FOURTEEN

CRYPTOGRAPHY

Labs included in this chapter:

➤ Lab 14.1 Installing a Certificate Server

➤ Lab 14.2 Installing a Client Certificate

➤ Lab 14.3 Administering a Certificate Server

➤ Lab 14.4 Managing Personal Certificates

➤ Lab 14.5 Managing Certificate Revocation

CompTIA Security+ Exam Objectives	
Objective	Lab
Basics of Cryptography: PKI: Certificates	14.1, 14.2, 14.3, 14.4, 14.5

LAB 14.1 INSTALLING A CERTIFICATE SERVER

Objectives

Servers running certificate services can perform as one of two types of certificate authorities: Enterprise or Stand-alone. The Enterprise CA is part of Active Directory and has the ability to use templates and smart cards, and to publish certificates in Active Directory. The Stand-alone CA does not require Active Directory and has no way to use templates. All certificates are marked pending until issued by an administrator. Certificates created on a Stand-alone CA are not published and therefore have to be distributed manually. In this lab you will install Certificate Services and create a Stand-alone Root CA that is not a member of a Windows 2000 domain.

After completing this lab, you will be able to:

➤ Install Windows 2000 Certificate Services

➤ Configure a Stand-alone root CA

Materials Required

This lab will require the following:

➤ A Windows 2000 server

➤ A Windows 2000 Server CD-ROM

Estimated completion time: **20–25 minutes**

ACTIVITY

1. Log on to your server as Administrator.

2. Click **Start**, **Settings**, **Control Panel**.

3. Double-click **Add/Remove Programs**.

4. Click **Add/Remove Windows Components**.

5. Select **Certificate Services**.

6. Click **Yes** to accept the warning message.

7. Click **Next**.

8. If necessary, select **Stand-alone root CA**, as shown in Figure 14-1.

9. Click **Next**.

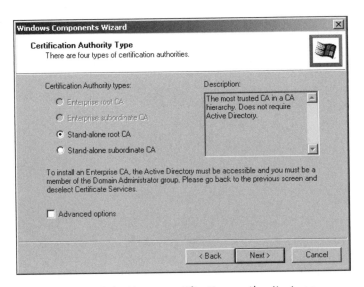

Figure 14-1   Selecting a certification authority type

10. Enter the information shown in Figure 14-2.

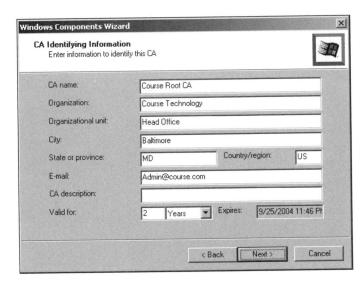

Figure 14-2   CA identifying information

11. Click **Next**.

12. Change the **Shared** folder to **C:\CertConfig** and then click **Next**.

13. Click **Yes** to create the share.

14. Click **OK** to stop IIS.

15. You may be prompted for the Windows 2000 Server CD. If so, insert the CD-ROM and press **Enter**.

16. Click **Finish**.

17. Close all windows and log off Administrator.

Certification Objectives

Objectives for CompTIA Security+ Exam:

➤ Basics of Cryptography: PKI: Certificates

Review Questions

1. Which of the following is best described as undeniable proof that a correspondence was sent or received?

   a. nonrepudiation

   b. return receipt

   c. mutual authentication

   d. verification

2. Which of the following uses a single key to encrypt and decrypt?

   a. public key

   b. symmetric key

   c. private key

   d. all of the above

3. Which of the following uses pair of keys to encrypt and decrypt?

   a. public key

   b. symmetric key

   c. private key

   d. all of the above

4. Which of the following is a feature of a Stand-alone CA?

   a. It is always trusted by all users and computers in its domain.

   b. It can use smart cards.

   c. It publishes certificates in Active Directory.

   d. none of the above

5. You can install a Stand-alone CA on a server that participates in an Active Directory organization. True or False?

LAB 14.2 INSTALLING A CLIENT CERTIFICATE

Objectives

Windows 2000 running certificate services and IIS have the ability to allow Web-based certificate requests. You can specify the type of certificate that you want and then wait for approval from an Administrator. If you were using an Enterprise CA, the approval process would be automatic. Because you are using a Standalone CA, however, the certificate is pending until approved. All of these steps can be performed using a Web browser and the certificate authority MMC snap-in. In this lab you will create a certificate request, issue the certificate, and install it.

After completing this lab, you will be able to:

➤ Request a client certificate

➤ Install a client certificate

Materials Required

This lab will require the following:

➤ A Windows 2000 server

➤ A Stand-alone CA

Estimated completion time: **20–25 minutes**

ACTIVITY

1. Log on to your server as Administrator.

2. Right-click **My Computer** and select **Manage**.

3. Expand **Local Users and Groups**.

4. Right-click **Users** and select **New User**.

5. Enter the name **CertUserX** in the User name field.

6. Click **Create**.

7. Enter **NoCertUserX** in the User name field.

8. Click **Create**.

9. Click **Close**.

10. Since you will log onto a stand-alone server make both users a member of the **Power Users Group**.

11. Close all Windows and log off.

14

12. Log on as CertUserX. You may be prompted to change your password.

13. Click **OK**, and then click **OK** again to keep the existing null password.

14. Launch Internet Explorer.

15. Enter **http://server-x\certsrv** in the address box then press Enter. You will see a screen resembling the one shown in Figure 14-3. Note: Replace *server-x* with the name of your server.

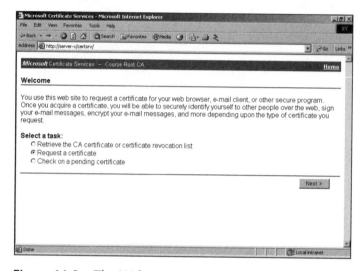

Figure 14-3   The Welcome screen when requesting a certificate

16. Accept the default task to **Request a Certificate**.

17. Click **Next**.

18. Click the **Advanced request** radio button.

19. Click **Next**.

20. Accept the default to **Submit a certificate request to this CA using a form**.

21. Click **Next**.

22. Change the length of the encryption key in the Key Size text box to **1024** and click the **Mark keys as exportable** check box, as shown in Figure 14-4.

23. Click **Submit**.

24. Log off CertUserX.

25. Log on Administrator.

26. Click **Start**, **Programs**, **Administrative Tools**, **Certification Authority**.

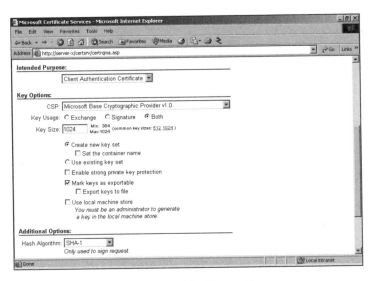

Figure 14-4   Certificate specification options

27. Expand **Course Root CA** and select **Pending Requests**, as shown in Figure 14-5.

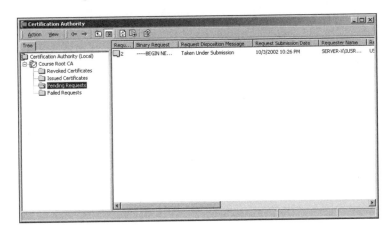

Figure 14-5   Issued certificates

28. Right-click the **Certificate**, select **All Tasks**, and then click **Issue**.

29. Log off Administrator.

30. Log on CertUserX.

31. Launch Internet Explorer.

32. Enter **http://server-x\certsrv** in the address box, and then press **Enter**
    Note: Replace *server-x* with the name of your server.

33. Click the **Check on a pending certificate** radio button, as shown in Figure 14-6.

14

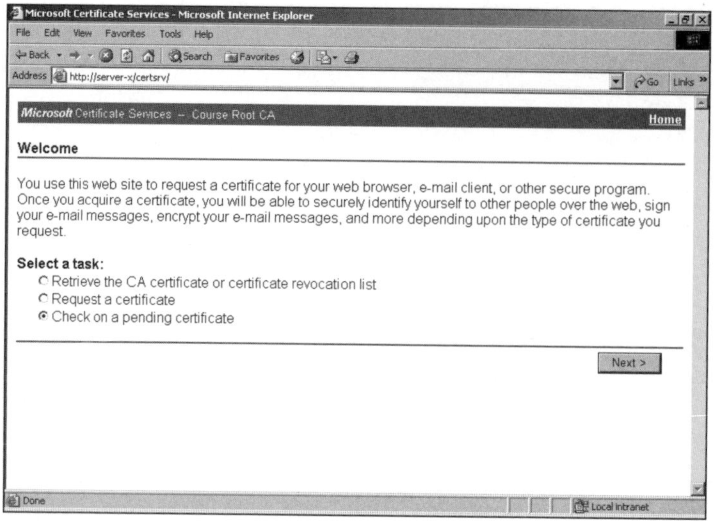

Figure 14-6 Check on a pending certificate

34. Click **Next**.

35. Select your certificate, and then click **Next**.

36. Click **Install this certificate**. You will receive a message that the certificate was successfully installed.

37. Close all windows and log off.

Certification Objectives

Objectives for CompTIA Security+ Exam:

➤ Basics of Cryptography: PKI: Certificates

Review Questions

1. What is the maximum Key Length for Microsoft PKI components?

   a. 512 bits

   b. 1024 bits

   c. 2048 bits

   d. 4096 bits

2. What is the maximum Key Length for some non-Microsoft PKI components?

   a. 512 bits

   b. 1024 bits

   c. 2048 bits

   d. 4096 bits

3. Which of the following is an example of a Hash Algorithm?

   a. MD4

   b. MD5

   c. SHA-1

   d. all of the above

4. By default, certificates are valid for _____.

   a. one month

   b. one year

   c. two years

   d. two months

5. Certificates that have special characters in the organization name have to be encoded in Unicode to remain compliant with the X.509 standard. True or False?

LAB 14.3 ADMINISTERING A CERTIFICATE SERVER

Objectives

Once you have the certificate authority up and running you should be sure to perform preventive maintenance. You have the ability to stop and start the service without shutting down the server, which can help reduce downtime while troubleshooting a problem. You also have the ability to back up and restore the CA. This is a critical part of preventive maintenance, especially if you have a hardware failure and lose the CA. The CA can be backed up with Windows 2000 Backup or the integrated backup program that is part of the certificate services. These backups can be completed without stopping the service, but the restore requires a reboot. In this lab, you will stop and start the certificate services and perform a backup and restore.

After completing this lab, you will be able to:

> ➤ Stop and start the Certificate Authority

> ➤ Back up and restore a Certificate Authority

Materials Required

This lab will require the following:

> ➤ A Windows 2000 server

> ➤ A Stand-alone root CA

> ➤ Administrator access to the server

14

Estimated completion time: **20–25 minutes**

ACTIVITY

1. Log on as Administrator.

2. Click **Start**, **Programs**, **Administrative Tools**, and select **Certification Authority**.

3. Right-click the **Course Root CA** and select **All Tasks**, **Stop Service**.

4. Once the Service has stopped, repeat Step 3 and click **Start Service**.

5. Create a folder named **C:\CABackup**.

6. Right-click the **Course Root CA** and select **All Tasks**, **Backup CA**.

7. Click **Next** to begin the Certificate Authority Backup Wizard.

8. Check the boxes for the items you wish to back up and enter the path, as shown in Figure 14-7.

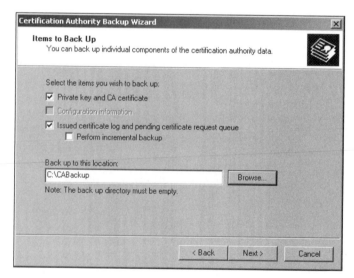

Figure 14-7 Items to back up

9. Click **Next**.

10. Enter **password** in the Password and Confirm password fields.

11. Click **Next**.

12. Click **Finish**.

13. Confirm that the backup was successful by looking at the following files: the **Course Root CA.p12** file in the CABackup folder, and **certback.dat**, **edb00001.log**, **Course Root CA.pat**, **Course Root CA.edb** in the Database folder.

14. Right-click the **Course Root CA** and select **All Tasks, Restore CA**.

15. Click **OK** to stop Certificate Services.

16. Click **Next**.

17. Check all boxes to restore everything.

18. Browse to the **C:\CABackup** folder.

19. Click **Next**.

20. Enter **password** for the password and click **Next**.

21. Click **Finish**.

22. Click **Yes** to restart certificate services.

23. Restart the server to finalize the settings.

Certification Objectives

Objectives for CompTIA Security+ Exam:

➤ Basics of Cryptography: PKI: Certificates

Review Questions

1. If your certificate authority hardware crashes, you will lose the ability to _____.

   a. issue certificates

   b. revoke certificates

   c. renew certificates

   d. all of the above

2. The certificate authority service must be stopped to perform a backup using the Certificate Authority Backup Wizard. True or False?

3. Which of the following is only available to back up in a Stand-alone CA environment?

   a. private key and CA certificate

   b. configuration information

   c. Issued Certificate Log and pending certificate request queue

   d. all of the above

14

4. Public key cryptology is also known as _____.

   a. PGP

   b. 3DES

   c. Diffie-Hellman

   d. RSA

5. The Data Encryption Standard (DES) uses a _____-bit key.

   a. 48

   b. 56

   c. 128

   d. 168

LAB 14.4 MANAGING PERSONAL CERTIFICATES

Objectives

There may be a time when you need to import or export your certificates. For instance, you may want to export a certificate for a backup or to use on another computer, or you may want to import a certificate for a restore or if it were sent to you by another user or computer. The file format used by Windows 2000 is Personal Information Exchange (PKCS#12). This file type enables the transfer of certificates and their key from one computer to another. In this lab you will export and import a certificate.

After completing this lab, you will be able to:

➤ Export a certificate

➤ Import a certificate

Materials Required

This lab will require the following:

➤ A Windows 2000 server

➤ A Stand-alone root CA

Estimated completion time: **15–20 minutes**

ACTIVITY

To prepare to export a certificate:

1. Log on to your server as Administrator.

2. Click **Start**, **Run**, and then type **mmc** and press **Enter**.

3. Click **Console, Add/Remove Snap-in**.

4. Click **Add**.

5. Click **Certificates**.

6. Click **Add**, select **My user account**, then click **Finish**.

7. Click **Close**, and then click **OK**.

8. Expand **Certificates – Current User**.

9. Expand **Personal**, and then click on **Certificates**, as shown in Figure 14-8.

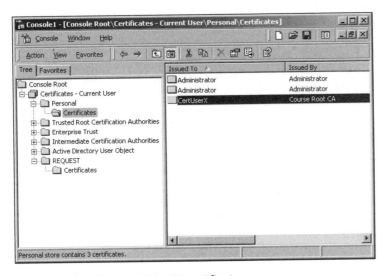

Figure 14-8   The CertUserX certificate

10. View the certificate for CertUserX by double-clicking the name.

11. Click **OK** to close the window.

To Export a certificate:

1. Right-click the **CertUserX** certificate.

2. Select **All Tasks**, and then click **Export**.

3. Click **Next** to begin the Certificate Export Wizard.

4. Click **Next** and accept the default options **Yes, export the private key** and **Enable strong protection**.

5. Select the **Personal Information Exchange PKCS#12** file format, and then click **Next**.

6. Enter **password** in the Password and Confirm password fields, and then click **Next**.

14

7. Enter **CertUserX** for the name of the file.

8. Click **Next**.

9. Click **Finish**.

10. Click **OK**.

To Import a certificate:

1. Launch Windows Explorer.

2. Navigate to **C:**.

3. Right-click the **CertUserX.pfx** file.

4. Click **Install PFX**.

5. Click **Next** to begin the wizard.

6. Click **Next** to accept the default file to import. Note: The name is in the 8.3 format, as shown in Figure 14-9.

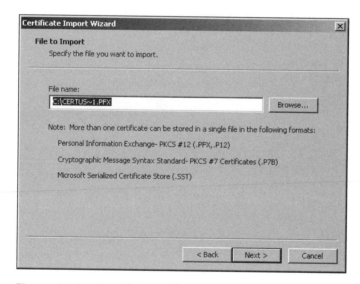

Figure 14-9   Specifying a file to import

7. Enter **password** in the Password field.

8. Click **Next**.

9. Click **Next** to accept the default **Certificate Store**.

10. Click **Finish**.

11. Click **OK**.

12. Close all windows and log off Administrator.

Certification Objectives

Objectives for CompTIA Security+ Exam:

➤ Basics of Cryptography: PKI: Certificates

Review Questions

1. Which of the following is the most widely used standard for digital certificates?

   a. X.400

   b. X.500

   c. X.25

   d. X.509

2. You can safely distribute your public key to others. True or False?

3. A third party certificate authority is always external to a company. True or False?

4. Which of the following certificate file formats are supported by Windows 2000? (Choose all that apply.)

   a. PKCS#12

   b. PKCS#7

   c. DER Encoded Binary X.500

   d. Base64 Encoded X.509

5. If another person wants to send you encrypted mail they must have your _____.

   a. private key

   b. public key

   c. S/MIME key

   d. all of the above

14

LAB 14.5 MANAGING CERTIFICATE REVOCATION

Objectives

Certificates are used to provide a way to verify the identity of individuals on a network. However, they are not 100% effective and can be compromised at times. Because of this, you need the ability to revoke certificates. Revoking certificates is an easy process that allows you to revoke the certificate and specify a reason for the revocation. In this lab you will revoke a certificate and evaluate the results.

After completing this lab, you will be able to:

➤ Revoke a certificate

➤ View the Certificate Revocation List

Materials Required

This lab will require the following:

➤ A Windows 2000 server with Certificate Services installed

➤ Administrator access to the server

Estimated completion time: **20–25 minutes**

ACTIVITY

1. Log on as Administrator.

2. Click **Start**, **Programs**, **Administrative Tools**, **Certification Authority**.

3. Expand **Course Root CA**.

4. Click **Issued Certificates**.

5. Right-click the **CertUserX** certificate and select **All Tasks**, **Revoke Certificate**.

6. Select **Key Compromise** for the reason, as shown in Figure 14-10.

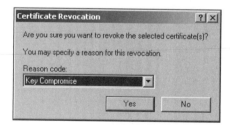

Figure 14-10   Specifying a reason for certificate revocation

7. Click **Yes**.

8. Click **Revoked Certificates**. Notice that the CertUserX certificate is in that folder.

9. Right-click **Revoked Certificates**, **All Tasks**, and then click **Publish**. If prompted, click **Yes** to publish a new CRL.

10. Click **OK**.

11. Right-click **Revoked Certificates**, and then select **Properties**.

12. Click **View Current CRL**.

13. View the contents of the General and Revocation List tabs to verify that the certificate was revoked.

14. Close all windows and log off Administrator.

Certification Objectives

Objectives for CompTIA Security+ Exam:

➤ Basics of Cryptography: PKI: Certificates

Review Questions

1. Which of the following is a reason to revoke a certificate?

   a. The key was lost.

   b. The key is known to someone else.

   c. The key has been compromised.

   d. all of the above

2. Once you revoke a certificate using Windows 2000 Certificate Services, it cannot be recovered. True or False?

3. In January 2001, _____ issued two fraudulent certificates to individuals claiming to be Microsoft.

   a. Verisign

   b. Sun

   c. Microsoft

   d. Entrust.net

4. Because of fraudulent certificates, it is safer to host an internal certificate authority than an external certificate authority. True or False?

5. Once you install Certificate services, you can not change the name of the computer if it is a Stand-alone or Enterprise Server. True or False?

14

PHYSICAL SECURITY

CompTIA Security+ Exam Objectives	
Objective	Lab
Operational/Organizational Security: Physical Security: Access Control	15.1, 15.2
Operational/Organizational Security: Physical Security: Environment	15.3
Operational/Organizational Security: Physical Security: Social Engineering	15.4

LAB 15.1 PHYSICAL BARRIERS

Objectives

To maintain security in your building, the perimeter of the facility needs to be secured. Gating and lock systems are the primary method for establishing a secure building. In an ideal world, a single point of entry will be used to "herd" all traffic into the facility. However, this is not the case with most companies. In most cases there are multiple points of entry into a building. The information security professional must utilize a "cat-burglar viewpoint" when surveying a site for physical vulnerabilities — starting with the perimeter. In the activity to follow, you will have an opportunity to put your cat-burglar viewpoint to work, to see if you can identify exterior perimeter vulnerabilities.

After completing this lab, you will be able to:

➤ Establish physical barriers to protect a facility

➤ Diagnose weaknesses in physical barrier protection for a facility

Materials Required

This lab will require the following:

➤ Paper and pen or pencil

➤ Visio flow chart software

Estimated completion time: **45–60 minutes**

ACTIVITY

Determining the perimeter strength of a site is also known as taking a Site Survey. This process requires some physical interaction on the part of the information security professional, who must physically examine the various points of entry to the facility and determine their weaknesses or strengths.

For this lab activity, you are to arrive at a local public facility of your choice and visually observe the physical barriers in place. Some examples of a public facility include the public library or town hall, a local grocery store, or a local retail store. You can perform your Site Survey by walking or driving around the facility. When you have finished your observations, draw a rough map of the grounds. Indicate the location of any fencing, gates, main entrance, side entrances, and loading docks. When you return to the classroom, use Visio to prepare a report / diagram of the physical barriers.

Do not exceed posted or nonposted trespassing rules of the facility. If you are not certain whether or not you are permitted in a particular location, do not go there.

At the completion of this activity, share your results with the class for discussion:

1. Take turns drawing your surveillance map on the white board, or distribute your Visio drawings to your classmates.

2. What perimeter weaknesses did you observe?

3. What perimeter strengths did you observe?

4. What would you change? Not change?

5. Would you want to keep your personal information in this facility? Why or why not?

Certification Objectives

Objectives for CompTIA Security+ Exam:

➤ Operational/Organizational Security: Physical Security: Access Control

Review Questions

1. Which of the following is a preventative physical barrier?

   a. fences/gates

   b. selection of a nonshared facility

   c. security guard patrols

   d. all of the above

2. Which of the following is a reactive physical security control?

   a. biometric devices

   b. sign–in log

   c. mantrap entrances

   d. all of the above

3. Which of the following is the most expensive physical security control?

   a. procedural controls

   b. hardware devices

   c. electronic systems

   d. personnel

4. Which of the following measures provides a first line of defense against potential risks and threats to a computer center?

   a. application security

   b. data security

   c. physical security

   d. telecommunications security

15

5. What should be done first, when a fire has been detected in a facility?

    a. Activate the fire suppression system.

    b. Evacuate the building.

    c. Call the fire department.

    d. Use fire extinguishers to put out the fire.

LAB 15.2 BIOMETRICS

Objectives

Biometrics is a security control that identifies an individual based on the examination of personal attributes, such as voiceprints or fingerprints. This type of high-tech authentication is often seen in movie theatres and is actually becoming more and more common place in secure facilities. The secure storage of authentication data is the key to preventing inappropriate access. The main benefit of biometrics is that it is not easy to exploit biometric authentication systems at the point of authentication.

After completing this lab, you will be able to:

➤ Understand appropriate uses for biometric technology

➤ Identify challenges associated with biometric technology

Materials Required

This lab will require the following:

➤ A computer with Internet access

Estimated completion time: **15–20 minutes**

ACTIVITY

Since biometrics is still an actively evolving technology, access to such devices is somewhat limited. However, manufacturers are competing to position themselves as leaders in the race to present biometrics authentication devices in a cost-effective and technologically effective manner. This activity requires Internet research to determine the current OEM leaders in biometric devices. Your tasks are as follows:

1. Search the Internet to identify biometrics OEMs.

2. Record the names of vendors that are leading the biometric systems marketplace right now.

3. What, if any, are the vulnerability(ies) associated with these devices?

Certification Objectives

Objectives for CompTIA Security+ Exam:

➤ Operational/Organizational Security: Physical Security: Access Control

Review Questions

1. Which of the following is an example of a biometric device?

   a. single-factor authentication

   b. multi-factor authentication

   c. retinal scanner

   d. proximity badge

2. Which of the following authenticates a user's access based on a personal identi-fication factor?

   a. biometrics

   b. access badge

   c. password

   d. lock

3. Biometrics is widely used to protect personal desktop computers. True or False?

4. Which of the following is the most reliable biometric authentication technique?

   a. password

   b. fingerprint

   c. voice verification

   d. iris scan

5. A retinal scan is a scan of the:

   a. eye

   b. face

   c. voice

   d. palm

15

LAB 15.3 ENVIRONMENT

Objectives

There are many components to managing a safe and secure environment. They range from fire protection and perimeter protection, to humidity and temperature controls. Regardless of the particular environment component being addressed by the security professional, the first and foremost concern always comes back to the safety of personnel.

This lab will focus on the considerations for establishing escape routes and fire suppression. When managing the control factors relating to fire suppression, the security professional should consider the following:

➤ Potential fuel sources for fire — oxygen and combustible materials that are kept in your facility

➤ Building contents — determine what dangerous or combustible materials are present in your facility, and how they may best be extinguished in case of fire

➤ Fire detection — the quicker that a fire is detected, the greater the opportunity to safely evacuate the premises and minimize the damage

➤ Fire extinguishing — Fire suppression comes in many forms, including sprinkler systems, halon systems, fire extinguishers, and water. Determine the best systems for your facility, depending on what materials are stored there.

After completing this lab, you will be able to:

➤ Establish fire suppression controls to protect a facility

➤ Diagnose weaknesses in fire suppression protection for a facility

Materials Required

This lab will require the following:

➤ Paper and pen or pencil

➤ Visio flow chart software

Estimated completion time: 45–60 minutes

ACTIVITY

This activity is another field trip. Take a walking tour of your school (or other public facility) with paper and pencil in hand. Your goal is to draw a rough draft of the floor plan. On the floor plan, indicate the location of sprinkler heads, fire extinguishers, and fire alarm triggers. For each fire extinguisher, take note of the next/last inspection date. Verify that it is up to date with inspections. At the completion of this activity, share your results with the class for discussion.

1. Take turns drawing your surveillance map on the white board, or distribute your Visio diagrams to the class.

2. What fire suppression controls did you observe?

3. Were the fire suppression controls adequate?

4. What would you change? Not change?

5. Would you feel safe in this facility?

Certification Objectives

Objectives for CompTIA Security+ Exam:

➤ Operational/Organizational Security: Physical Security: Environment

Review Questions

1. Electrical fires are classified as:

   a. class A fires

   b. class B fires

   c. class C fires

   d. class D fires

2. Which of the following is an appropriate control in a computer room?

   a. smoke detection equipment that shuts down the wet pipe equipment

   b. smoke detection equipment that shuts down the air conditioning equipment

   c. smoke detection equipment that shuts down the UPS

   d. smoke detection equipment that shuts down the badge access controls

3. Where is the best place to sound an alarm from a computer center?

   a. receptionist desk

   b. guard station

   c. fire and police station

   d. CEO's office

4. What instrument is used to measure humidity levels in a computer center?

   a. hydrometer

   b. hygrometer

   c. barometer

   d. voltmeter

5. The most important asset to protect in a facility is the computer center. True or False?

15

LAB 15.4 SOCIAL ENGINEERING

Objectives

Social engineering refers to the act of tricking someone into divulging their password or information about network vulnerabilities. This is often done by pretending to be someone you are not in order to gain some level of access that you should not have. Other components of social engineering include eavesdropping and snooping in places where you should not be. In general, people are the weakest link in the information security field. At some level we all have a desire to help others, and we often are quick to provide answers to questions that we should sometimes be wary of. Another careless tactic that people often overlook is the privacy and protection of their retired items (otherwise known as trash). That's right: one man's trash really is a hacker's treasure. The following two activities will help you hone your social engineering skills, and then apply them to educating others on good common sense actions.

After completing this lab, you will be able to:

➤ Improve your personal information protection habits

➤ Educate others on best practices for defending social engineering attacks

Materials Required

This lab will require the following:

➤ Paper and pen or pencil

Estimated completion time: **45–60 minutes**

ACTIVITY

Active Listening

Active listening, or eavesdropping, simply requires your attention. Over a period of one week you will hear an amazing amount of information—if you listen. Your first task is to keep a diary of private information that you hear your friends, family, fellow students, and co-workers say. For example, in an office environment with cubicles, your co-workers will often have conversations that are far too revealing. Maybe they are refinancing their home, so they give out their social security number, or perhaps you hear them give their account number to their bank over the phone.

After accruing this list, your second task is to come clean and let them know what you have heard and explain to them that they need to be more careful with their private conversations. At the completion of this activity, share your results with your class for discussion, omitting the private information you have collected.

Snooping

Another component of social engineering is snooping. For this activity, get ready to roll up your sleeves and get dirty—literally. It's time to do a little trash picking. Your goal is to take one bag of your trash and go through it, to see what a hacker might use to gain access to your private, electronic information. That's right, take a bag of trash that you were going to put out for pickup and empty it out. Examples of what you might find include bills with account numbers, bank statements, old checks, important documents with your social security number on them, and much more. Discuss your findings with your classmates.

Certification Objectives

Objectives for CompTIA Security+ Exam:

➤ Operational/Organizational Security: Physical Security: Social Engineering

Review Questions

1. What kind of attack is used to persuade a user or administrator into giving out information or access?

   a. DDOS attack

   b. social engineering attack

   c. Syn attack

   d. all of the above

2. Social engineering requires strong technical skills. True or False?

3. Who is susceptible to a social engineering attack?

   a. CEO

   b. system administrator

   c. Help Desk

   d. all of the above

4. Which is the best tactic to prevent social engineering?

   a. training and awareness programs

   b. strong policies

   c. Threaten to fire employees who give out information.

   d. Install surveillance systems.

5. How should you securely dispose of secure documents?

   a. Use a vertical shredder.

   b. Use a cross-shredder.

   c. Tear the document into pieces.

   d. Cross out private information and throw the document away.

15

CHAPTER SIXTEEN

DISASTER RECOVERY AND BUSINESS CONTINUITY

Labs included in this chapter:
➤ Lab 16.1 Creating Security Policies

CompTIA Security+ Exam Objectives	
Objective	**Lab**
Operational/Organizational Security: Policy and Procedures: Security Policy	16.1

CASE STUDY: ACME CLEANSERS

Background

You have just been hired as a Network Security Analyst for Acme Cleansers, a large company specializing in the manufacture of a unique cleaning product. This company has 10,000 employees worldwide and is continuing to grow every year. Management has decided to hire a security expert because a few recent security breaches have caused significant company downtime. The most recent event was a DDOS attack that prevented customers from purchasing for two full days. Over the past year this company has had over 10 days of downtime due to similar attacks. Even though the company is very profitable, this downtime has resulted in a large number of unhappy clients. Your job is to evaluate the current situation and make recommendations to the existing IT management staff. You have decided to follow these steps:

> ➤ Document the current security configurations.

> ➤ Interview management and employees from each department.

> ➤ Recommend a security policy.

During the documentation phase you discovered:

> ➤ The company has a firewall, but it is not configured properly.

> ➤ The company has virus scanning software on all of the desktops, and the signatures are managed by the individual users.

> ➤ The company has a single Windows 2000 domain with 11 sites with the following properties:

> - The file systems are a mix of FAT32 and NTFS.
> - All users are local administrators.
> - No Windows security policies exist, not even a password policy.
> - Auditing is not enabled.
> - Internet access is not monitored or filtered.
> - E-mail is not protected with virus protection software.

During the interview phase you discovered:

> ➤ Employees have not been trained on the basics of computer security.

> ➤ Most employees are using blank passwords.

> ➤ Employees spend an average of two hours per day casually surfing the Internet. (Note: if they are willing to admit to two hours, it is most likely closer to four hours.)

➤ Most employees have lost data because of a virus outbreak.

➤ Employees have access to the company network by using their personal ISP and a VPN connection. The VPN uses PPTP with PAP authentication.

During the recommendation phase you decided:

➤ To submit a document that summarizes your findings

➤ To create a basic security policy template in specific areas for the company so that the company can maintain and expand the policy in the future

LAB 16.1 CREATING SECURITY POLICIES

Objectives

Setting security policies is an important first step in securing the data in your organization. In addition to making it more difficult for hackers to infiltrate your defenses, security policies promote good habits in your end users. In this lab you will create security policies relating to various aspects of your network.

After completing this lab, you will be able to:

➤ Create an overall security policy with:

- An Acceptable Use Policy

- A Password Protection Policy

- A Remote Access Policy

- An Anti-Virus Process

- A VPN Security Policy

Materials Required

This lab will require the following:

➤ A Windows 2000 server with Internet access

16

Estimated completion time: **90 minutes**

ACTIVITY

1. Visit the SANS Institute Web site and create a simple security policy for the company in the scenario above. This site is located at the following URL: *www.sans.org/newlook/resources/policies/policies.htm*.

2. Review the SANS security policy primer at: *www.sans.org/newlook/resources/policies/Policy_Primer.pdf*.

3. Create a document reporting your findings about the current state of security at Acme Cleansers for the board of directors.

4. Create a security policy for the following areas using the templates at: *www.sans.org/newlook/resources/policies/policies.htm#template.*

- Acceptable Use Policy
- Password Protection Policy
- Remote Access Policy
- Anti-Virus Process
- VPN Security Policy

Certification Objectives

Objectives for CompTIA Security+ Exam:

➤ Operational/Organizational Security: Policy and Procedures: Security Policy

Review Questions

1. Which of the following trust models is the most restrictive?
   a. Trust everyone all of the time.
   b. Trust no one at any time.
   c. Trust some people some of the time.
   d. none of the above

2. Which of the following trust models is the easiest to enforce?
   a. Trust everyone all of the time.
   b. Trust no one at any time.
   c. Trust some people some of the time.
   d. none of the above

3. Which of the following trust models gives access as needed?
   a. Trust everyone all of the time.
   b. Trust no one at any time.
   c. Trust some people some of the time.
   d. none of the above

4. Policies have the greatest effect on _____.
   a. managers
   b. users
   c. IT Staff
   d. auditors

5. Categorize each of the following as either "M" (what policies must do) or "S" (what policies should do).

   a. Describe what is covered by the policies ——————————

   b. State reasons why the policy is needed ——————————

   c. Be implemented and enforceable ——————————

   d. Define contacts and responsibilities ——————————

   e. Be concise and easy to understand ——————————

   f. Balance protection with productivity ——————————

   g. Discuss how violations will be handled ——————————

6. You must have management support to be able to implement a security policy. True or False?

7. Which of the following defines and describes the appropriate use of resources?

   a. remote access

   b. information protection

   c. perimeter security

   d. acceptable use

   e. none of the above

8. Which of the following defines and describes acceptable methods of connecting to an internal network from an outside source?

   a. remote access

   b. information protection

   c. perimeter security

   d. acceptable use

   e. none of the above

9. Which of the following defines and describes how physical security is maintained?

   a. remote access

   b. information protection

   c. perimeter security

   d. acceptable use

   e. none of the above

16

10. Which backup method is equivalent to a Full backup?

   a. level 0

   b. level 1

   c. level 2

   d. level 3

11. Arrange the following incident response categories in the order of completion when there is a virus incident:

    a. Identify the problem.

    b. Isolate the system.

    c. Notify the necessary people.

12. Who should be on a security committee when determining the security policy requirements?

    a. management

    b. IT staff

    c. users

    d. all of the above

13. Which of the following are reasons for resistance to security policies? (Choose all that apply.)

    a. Employees do not like change.

    b. Security policies are illegal.

    c. a fear of be spied on

    d. all of the above

14. Which of the following is a level 1 security incident?

    a. sharing of user accounts

    b. computer virus infection

    c. employee termination

    d. abuse of access privileges

15. Which of the following is a level 3 security incident?

    a. sharing of user accounts

    b. computer virus infection

    c. employee termination

    d. abuse of access privileges

COMPUTER FORENSICS AND ADVANCED TOPICS

Labs included in this chapter:
➤ Lab 17.1 Performing Risk Analysis

CompTIA Security+ Exam Objectives	
Objective	**Lab**
Operational/Organizational Security: Risk Identification	17.1

CASE STUDY: ACME BOOKS

Background

You are an IT manager for Acme Books, an e-commerce company that competes with Amazon.com. You are trying to justify the implementation of security and disaster recovery upgrades. This company has 5,000 employees with three offices in North America in New York, Los Angeles, and Montreal, and two offices overseas, in London and Paris. You recently experienced problems with the hardware and software used to run the e-commerce site. These problems resulted in 15 hours of downtime during prime business hours. Upper management sent you a message asking you to explain why the problems are occurring and encouraging you to prevent these events in the future. You feel that it is a good time to perform risk analysis for the company. You have decided to follow these steps:

- ➤ Identify the knowledge level of all employees in the company.
- ➤ Determine security requirements.
- ➤ Identify vulnerabilities.
- ➤ Develop a protection plan.

During the knowledge phase you discovered the following:

- ➤ Upper management is aware of the cost of downtime.
- ➤ Upper management is not aware of why the downtime is occurring.
- ➤ Users are not aware of the cost associated with downtime.
- ➤ Users have been trained only on the sales software product and Microsoft Office.
- ➤ No one outside of the IT department understands the complex design of the e-commerce system.
- ➤ Customers are beginning to complain about downtime.

During the security requirement phase you discovered the following:

- ➤ A network diagram does not exist.
- ➤ Physical building security does not exist.
- ➤ Access to the network operations center is not controlled.
- ➤ The firewall service agreement was never used and is now expired.
- ➤ The virus scanning service agreement is also expired.

During the vulnerability phase you discovered the following:

- ➤ The firewall has not been updated for three years.
- ➤ Administrators use Telnet and FTP for remote access to the network servers.

➤ Users are local administrators of their PCs.

➤ Users have not been trained on the impact of computer viruses.

➤ Users have unknowingly installed spyware on their PCs.

➤ Some users have disabled their virus scanning software.

➤ Servers are not clustered or load balanced.

➤ The backup method is sufficient, but the tapes are located on site.

During the protection plan phase you decided to do the following:

➤ Submit a document that summarizes your risk analysis.

➤ Submit a plan to upgrade the necessary areas of the IT infrastructure.

LAB 17.1 PERFORMING RISK ANALYSIS

Objectives

A thorough analysis of the current state of the security on your network can help you identify weaknesses that may pose security risks. This analysis can serve many purposes. Identifying problem areas can show upper management the need to devote resources to the problem. This process can also help you focus your attention and resources in the most appropriate directions.

After completing this lab, you will be able to:

➤ Understand the complexity of risk analysis

➤ Create a risk analysis report using the OCTAVE method as a guide

Materials Required

This lab will require the following:

➤ A Windows 2000 server with Internet access

Estimated completion time: **90 minutes**

17

ACTIVITY

In this activity you will visit the CERT Web site and perform risk analysis for the company in the scenario above. The Web site can be found at the following URL: *www.cert.org*.

1. Review the introduction to the OCTAVE method at: *www.cert.org/octave/ methodintro.html*.

2. Using the OCTAVE method, create a risk analysis report for the following areas:
- Phase 1: Build Asset–Based Threat Profiles
  - Process 1: Identify Senior Management Knowledge
  - Process 2: Identify Operational Area Knowledge
  - Process 3: Identify Staff Knowledge
  - Process 4: Create Threat Profiles
- Phase 2: Identify Infrastructure Vulnerabilities
  - Process 5: Identify Key Components
  - Process 6: Evaluate Selected Components
- Phase 3: Develop Security Strategy and Plans
  - Process 7: Conduct Risk Analysis
  - Process 8: Develop Protection Strategy

Certification Objectives

Objectives for CompTIA Security+ Exam:

➤ Operational/Organizational Security: Risk Identification

REVIEW QUESTIONS

1. Arrange the following in the order of the forensic process:
   a. analysis
   b. collection
   c. examination
   d. preparation
   e. documentation

2. In network forensics, it is essential to keep track of the chain-of-custody when handling evidence. True or False?

3. When responding to an incident, which of the following would you perform?
   a. Examine log files.
   b. Look for sniffers.
   c. Look for remote control programs.
   d. Look for file sharing programs.
   e. all of the above

4. If you are under attack from a hacker, what should you do first?

   a. Observe the attacker.

   b. Chase the attacker away.

   c. Do a system backup.

   d. Catch the attacker.

5. If you want to prosecute an attacker, you should contact legal counsel immediately. True or False?

6. What is the primary reason most computer crimes go unpunished?

   a. education

   b. privacy issues

   c. lack of resources

   d. none of the above

7. What is it called when an attacker impersonates another system by using its IP address?

   a. DDOS

   b. IP spoofing

   c. IP splicing

   d. IP tampering

8. What is it called when an attacker denies legitimate users access to a system?

   a. DDOS

   b. IP spoofing

   c. IP splicing

   d. IP tampering

9. What is it called when an attacker hijacks an active session?

   a. DDOS

   b. IP spoofing

   c. IP splicing

   d. IP tampering

10. Which of the following stages of risk management is the first step?

   a. Monitoring

   b. Evaluation of Control

   c. Management

   d. Threat Assessment

   e. Inventory

17

11. In which of the following stages of risk management is a vulnerability list created?

   a. Monitoring

   b. Evaluation of Control

   c. Management

   d. Threat Assessment

   e. Inventory

12. Which of the following stages of risk management is ongoing as the process evolves?

   a. Monitoring

   b. Evaluation of Control

   c. Management

   d. Threat Assessment

   e. Inventory

13. What area of security management utilizes an IDS?

   a. Security Technology Management

   b. Vulnerability Management

   c. Systems Availability

14. What area of security management maintains a library of attack signatures?

   a. Security Technology Management

   b. Vulnerability Management

   c. Exploitation Management

   d. Systems Availability

15. Who is typically responsible for overseeing the risk management process?

   a. IT Manager

   b. Chief Executive Officer

   c. Chief Financial Office

   d. Chief Security Officer